*Faith Victorious in the
Kentucky Mountains*

Rev. Lela G. McConnell
President and Founder
of the
Kentucky Mountain Holiness Association

Faith Victorious

in the

Kentucky Mountains

★ ★ ★

THE STORY OF
TWENTY-TWO YEARS OF SPIRIT-FILLED
MINISTRY

BY

REV. LELA G. McCONNELL

Author of "The Pauline Ministry in the Kentucky Mountains"

Printed for the author
by
LIGHT AND LIFE PRESS
Winona Lake, Indiana
1946

Copyright, 1946
by
Lela G. McConnell

Printed in the United States of America

Gratefully Dedicated

To

The Household of Faith
Who May Be Helped in Any Degree
By Reading These Pages,

And to

The Donors and Prayer Partners
In this Work of Faith, including the
Mountain Missionary Society of Asbury College

TABLE OF CONTENTS

LIST OF ILLUSTRATIONS

PREFACE

For the past year, God has been laying it upon my heart to write another book. My first book, "*The Pauline Ministry In The Kentucky Mountains*" (nothing that appears there is repeated here, this being an entirely new book) has been truly used of the Lord. I have received thousands of letters telling me how God has honored it in helping the saints of God, and convicting the unsaved and unsanctified, so that many have been led to seek the Lord. I humbly give God all the glory.

I, therefore, feel led to put into permanent form more of the rich experiences and vindications of His Word in our Faith work in the Mountains of Eastern Kentucky.

At a time when an endless series of political conflicts make this earth such an uncomfortable place, and in a world troubled and beset by every kind of global strife and selfishness, and when men's very hearts are failing them for fear and uncertainty, it is a joy to write of the realities of Faith, and the sureties of our immutable God and His unchangeable promises. Acts 2: 26, "Therefore did my heart rejoice, and my tongue was glad."

I trust that the Lord will put His seal upon this volume for the encouragement of His children and the extension of His glorious kingdom.

I have asked my splendid corps of co-laborers to contribute to the book some of their rich experiences in faith, and also to tell about their calls.

Again, I am deeply grateful to dear Mr. and Mrs. C. Kildow Lovejoy for having me as their guest, as I write this book in another of the fine hotels of their Kildow Hotel Company. This volume is written at "The Governor Cabell" in Huntington, West Virginia. My first book was written in their hotel, "The Ritz" in Paducah, Kentucky. I know the Lord does reward them for this good kindness.

LELA G. McCONNELL

July 2, 1946
Lawson, Breathitt County, Kentucky

*Faith Victorious in the
Kentucky Mountains*

I

THE AUTHOR'S LIFE OF FAITH

"And when he was forty years old, it came into his heart. . . ." Acts 7: 23. Just as Moses was led of the Lord at the age of forty to go to Egypt, so truly did the Lord lead me into the hills of Eastern Kentucky in the fortieth year of my life. "So they being sent forth by the Holy Ghost departed. . . ." Acts 13: 4.

On June 1, 1924, my birthday, I left the campus of Asbury College with all my belongings (which were very few because of the great fire earlier that same year) to answer the call of God for the rest of my life. It was a very happy day for me. My soul was aflame with the joy of the Lord and the peace of God that passeth all understanding.

The good promises that were so rich and assuring to me then were: "For the Lord God is a sun and shield: the Lord will give grace and glory: no good thing will he withhold from them that walk uprightly." Psalm 84: 11. "Be strong and of a good courage, fear not: for the Lord thy God, He it is that doth go with thee: He will not fail thee, nor forsake thee." Deut. 31: 6. "And the Lord, He it is that doth go before thee; . . . fear not, neither be dismayed." Deut. 31: 8.

With no church back of me financially, it made me very dependent upon the Lord. He kept renewing these promises to me, and giving me new ones to stand upon, as I walked in the Light and followed the Lord closely. God kept pouring the blessings daily into my soul, so that the severe trials and hardships of the first year only proved to me more and more the truth of God's precious word. He was building into my soul depths of faith that I had not known before. I was afraid of nothing but the fear of grieving God or compromising. The Holy Ghost often brought to my mind, while in prayer, Heb. 11:33: "Who through faith subdued kingdoms, wrought righteousness, obtained promises, stopped the mouths of lions ... out of weakness were made strong, waxed valiant in fight, turned to flight the armies of the aliens."

However, this faith is not reached easily. In my childhood days, the Lord had taught me lessons of faith. My earliest recollections of faith in God I learned through my precious mother. Her trust in the Lord was very vital. Her prayers, God answered in a marked way.

I was in the fifth grade when one of my brothers ran away from home. At the family altar the next morning, my mother prayed *oh so tenderly and powerfully for him*. We children all cried until our hearts were nearly broken as mother poured out her heart to God. The following day my brother came humbly walking home. God had heard Mother's prayer.

When I was ten years old my father was wonderfully converted. He prayed and sought the Lord for

Birthplace of Lela G. McConnell
Honey Brook — Chester Co., Penn.

Miss McConnell at the age of 23

Mrs. Rebekah Martha Eshelman
McConnell—Mother of Author

days in a revival in our Methodist Church at Honey Brook, Pa. This, I knew, was in direct answer to Mother's prayers. I had often heard her pray for his salvation.

On Sunday afternoons my mother had *a religious service in the parlor of our farm house.* The neighbors and friends would come in. I recall so vividly how the rich blessing of the Lord was poured out upon the people as they sang and praised God.

My childish heart was made hungry to know the Lord as far back as I can remember. Conviction would sieze me and I would go and hide and pray for the Lord to help me and make me a good girl.

The songs which were sung so often in the Methodist Class Meeting where I attended with my father and mother were:

"Anywhere with Jesus I can safely go!
Anywhere He leads me in this world below!
Anywhere without Him dearest joys would fade—
Anywhere with Jesus, I am not afraid!

Anywhere! anywhere! Fear I cannot know;
Anywhere with Jesus I can safely go!"

"More, more about Jesus,
More, more about Jesus;
More of His saving fulness see,
More of His love who died for me."

These two songs made we want to be a Christian every time the saints sang them with power, bless-

ing and liberty. It was the joy of the Lord in their
hearts that made such a deep impression on me.
These songs, with the rich testimonies and shouts of
victory, were a great source of help to my ever-in-
creasing faith in God. I recall with deep gratitude
the family altar and Mother's prayers.

One day while I was walking along a country road
near our home, *I lost a quarter of a dollar.* I had
earned it by selling berries and its loss meant much
to me. I looked a long time but could not find it.
Finally, I asked the Lord to please help me to find it.
Instantly a voice said to me, "It is in the creek by the
side of the road." I looked and there I saw it shining
in the bottom of the water. I was not converted yet,
but the Lord used this to prove and strengthen my
faith in Him.

I cannot but thank God now that I had very little
of this world's goods around me as a child; also, that
I grew up on a farm. I was compelled to work hard.
Such early surroundings were a great blessing to
me, for they helped me to build up the power of perseverence and good character.

In my book, *"The Pauline Ministry in the Kentucky Mountains,"* I have related my life story and
told in detail my spiritual biography. I will not repeat it here. Suffice it to say, that the Lord saved me
at the age of thirteen in a revival in our Methodist
Church at Honey Brook, Pennsylvania, in January,
1898. "Therefore being justified by faith, we have
peace with God through our Lord Jesus Christ."
Rom. 5: 1. Six years later He sanctified me wholly

at the National Holiness Camp Meeting at Delanco, N. J., July 4, 1904.

Dr. G. W. Ridout was preaching from the Word about Christians who knew Jesus well, yet needed to have the carnal nature cleansed out of their hearts. I said, "Jesus, that's what I've been hungry for these six years since Thou hast saved me." I went to the altar. I sought for days. Finally, I said in my desperation, "Jesus, I must have the blessing now." Instantly, the Holy Ghost came and applied the Blood of Jesus to my carnal heart and cleansed out the old inbred sin. The rest mentioned in Hebrews 4: 9 was mine: "There remaineth therefore a rest to the people of God." The prayer of Jesus for His disciples was answered for me too. "They are not of the world, even as I am not of the world. Sanctify them through thy truth: thy word is truth. Neither pray I for these alone, but for them also which shall believe on me through their word; I in them, and Thou in me, that they may be made perfect in one; and that the world may know that Thou hast sent me, and hast loved them, as Thou hast loved me." John 17: 20, 23.

I have never ceased to praise God for the good seeking the Lord held me to when I wanted Him to forgive my sins. For three days I was repenting and confessing. At last my faith took hold of the promise, "If we confess our sins, he is faithful and just to forgive us our sins." I John 1: 9. My soul sang, "Oh happy day, when Jesus washed my sins away." I knew my name was written down in Glory. The burden of sins was gone.

Now, my heart, having been "justified by faith" and "sanctified by faith," was able to enjoy the great blessings of Calvary. The glory that filled my heart then has been mine through these years. The Canaan Land warfare grows richer and deeper all the time and my faith increases constantly.

Also I have been so grateful to the Lord for taking me to the bottom in my consecration when I was seeking for nearly ten days to be sanctified. The last thing was the unknown bundle. I know that the Lord saw many things that would need to be fought through as I walked on with Him. Thus I could say, "This was in the unknown bundle in my full consecration." This has made it easier to keep saying yes to all the will of God through these years. I came fully to the place, where, as John Wesley says, "Faith automatically works when all is on the altar." "The altar that sanctifieth the gift." Matt. 23: 19. The altar is Jesus and we are the gift. The Lord has kept me in His will so preciously through these forty-two years in the Canaan Land warfare. Often I say with the disciples, "Did not our hearts burn within us, while He talked with us by the way, and while He opened to us the Scriptures."

Thus God has permitted many marked providences to come into my life from early childhood, in order to prepare me better to take the many responsibilities that are mine today. "Except a corn of wheat fall into the ground and die, it abideth alone: but if it die it bringeth forth much fruit." John 12: 24. I'd a million times rather be where God wants me in a hard field and no pay, than be where God does not want me with good pay. To be supremely happy, satisfied, and contented, have enough to eat, to wear, and have a comfortable place to sleep is life in abundance. Beloved, to mind religion young saves us from a thousand snares. My year verse for 1937 was Mark 9: 23, "All things are possible to him that believeth."

Martin Luther said,

> "God's Word, for all their craft and force,
>   One moment shall not linger
> But, spite of hell, shall have its course;
>   'Tis written by His finger."

Our faith linked to God's love and power makes everything in the promises of God possible.

> "Laughs at impossibilities,
>   And cries, 'It shall be done.'"

When the disciples prayed, "Lord increase our faith," they were reproved for not possessing more faith and told how their faith was to be increased; namely, by serving faithfully with what they already possessed, and that *obedience is essential* to an increase of faith. "But which of you, having a servant plowing or feeding cattle, will say unto him by and by, when he is come from the field, Go and sit down to meat? And will not rather say unto him, Make ready wherewith I may sup, and gird thyself, and serve me, till I have eaten and drunken; and afterward thou shalt eat and drink? Doth he thank that servant because he did the things that were commanded him? I trow not. So likewise ye, when ye shall have done all those things which are commanded you, say, We are unprofitable servants: we have done that which was our duty to do." Luke 17: 7-10. Faith is increased not by divine bestowments, but by obedience to God's commands.

While I was growing up on the farm, my father had me stop at *the old blacksmith shop* in Cambridge, Chester County, Pennsylvania, on my way home from the creamery. I was impressed with the large muscle that stood out on the arm of the blacksmith. That man had the ability to strike the blows that developed his muscle. He didn't kneel down by his anvil to pray for an increase of muscle. No— he struck the iron day after day, faithfully and constantly. Thus upon his arm was formed not a muscle merely—he had that when he was a day old—but an increased muscle. He who has faith will work or his faith dies; he who works increases his faith. Therefore, faith puts the almighty power of God into the hands of men.

I was *clearly called to preach* in my early youth, but did not regard the call as from God until later. For many years after my conversion, I would weep and pray for God to give me courage to tell it; but I knew the prejudiced attitude of so many people toward women preachers. I would preach to myself while working alone on the farm. Sometimes at the end of a ten-acre field, when I would be harrowing the ground or raking the hay or hoeing corn, I would go to a fence corner and pray and get blest over the rich truths that the Lord would give to me.

Finally, at the age of twenty-three, He led me through Normal School and years of teaching school. I made it known and testified to God's call to preach because the burden had become too much to carry all alone. An intense conviction seized me, "Woe is unto me if I preach not the gospel." I Cor. 9:16. Only those who have gone through with such testings, know the battles of women preachers. However, the indescribable rest and assurance that this was God's will for me, gave me full courage to answer the call.

"And God is able to make all grace abound toward you; that ye, always having all sufficiency in all things, may abound to every good work." II Cor. 9:8. God gave to me strength constantly as I stood on the promise "Trust ye in the Lord forever: for in the Lord Jehovah is everlasting strength." Isa. 26:4. "Truly God is good to Israel, even to such as are of a clean heart." Psalm 73:1. "This book of the law shall not depart out of thy mouth; but thou shalt meditate therein day and night, that thou mayest observe to do according to all that is written therein: for then thou shalt make thy way prosperous, and then thou shalt have good success." Josh. 1:8.

Thus enjoying a vital heart experience in saving grace and in sanctifying power, I was enabled to trust God with a real and tangible faith. My faith was tested often and so the Lord increased it in preparation to answer His call to Eastern Kentucky. I was visiting my brother in Alberta, Canada, while he was homesteading. He slept in the barn and I stayed in the one-room shack by the side of the road. The barn was far from the road. I was *seized with a dreadful fear* one night. I could not sleep. Finally, I cried unto the Lord to take care of me and relieve me of the fear. Instantly, it all left me. God heard my prayer so that instantly I felt safe and blessed. The answer was quick and real. The joy of it all lingered with me for days. This lifted my faith in God in a new way.

I was pastor's assistant in Atlantic City, N. J., in the Central Methodist Church in 1917-18. I had to *trust God for many things.* I needed a watch, an umbrella, and a new Bible. I prayed for the Lord to lay this need on hearts, not telling anyone. In less than a month, the Lord moved on hearts to give me money so that I could buy a lovely good Bible, an umbrella and a watch. I never shall forget the joy that was mine for this definite answer to the prayer of faith.

I see now that the Lord was getting me ready to live by faith, and in the Kentucky Mountains. He took me through Chicago Evangelistic Institute and Asbury College on faith. I often thank God for the rugged way He permitted my faith to be tested and thus increased.

Further strengthening of my faith came through a most remarkable answer to prayer with reference to my mother. After the Lord laid it so heavily upon my heart to quit the public school room in Atlantic

City, N. J., where I was under tenure of office with a very good salary, and to give my entire time to Christian work, I faced one of the hardest problems of my life. My one sister was teaching away from home. The other one had given up her teaching job and was getting married and moving to Philadelphia to live. This meant that mother would have to live alone. The responsibility of her comfort weighed much upon me. The fact that she was enjoying the Canaan Land experience made it look so good that some day she and I would be living together, because we enjoyed the same spiritual fellowship.

When I settled it fully to follow God's plan to go into Christian service, unusual peace and joy flooded my soul. The day I left to go to the Chicago Evangelistic Institute in order to train for Christian service, mother was weeping when she said good by. Tenderly she said, "I will not put a straw in your way. Go, and mind the Lord and He will take care of me." I put her in the Lord's care and keeping. I trusted Him fully to work out a plan so that she would not need to live alone.

The school board of Honey Brook, where we lived, asked my older sister if she would accept a position to teach there. She had already contracted to return to the same school where she had been teaching. However, she resigned that position and signed the contract to teach the grades at home. This meant she would live with mother all the time. This was a very definite answer to prayer. If we truly want to mind God, He will take care of every perplexing

circumstance. "Let your requests be made known
unto God." Phil. 4: 6.

Study of God's word in the Chicago Evangelistic
Institute and in Asbury College, and reading the Bible through many times since, has given me a better
understanding of God's dealings and a keener insight into the devices of Satan, than I could have
had without such helps.

The Lord gave me many marked *answers to
prayer in my evangelistic years*. I was enabled,
through faith, to claim victory for souls to be saved
and sanctified in each revival. This was during the
years of 1919-22.

To win souls takes great faith; much greater than
faith for finances or material things. The enemy will
fight harder and hinder more when it comes to helping folks to get through to God, than he will fight
about faith for anything else. "Fear not, Daniel . . .
for thy words were heard, and I am come for thy
words. But the prince of the kingdom of Persia with-
stood me one and twenty days: but Michael, one of
the chief princes, came to help me." Dan. 10: 12, 13.

Often in my evangelistic work I met *opposition to
the truth of holiness*, yet the Lord sealed the messages to the satisfaction of many precious souls. This
sealing of my work gave me the the encouragement
I needed from time to time. My faith never wavered.
And the Lord helped me not to lower the standard
and kept me from ever compromising. In the early
days of my ministry, such opposition was hard to
understand because the Bible was so full of holiness,

and all the Protestant old-line churches had the doctrine of holiness in their disciplines. In fact, two-
thirds of the Word is written for us Christians; showing our need of holiness, how to get this blessing of
full salvation, the promises making provision for it,
and how to keep it. The Bible doctrine of entire
sanctification, as taught by John Wesley, has always
encountered opposition, but thank God, as time goes
on He has always raised up more and more intelli-
gent and valiant advocates to re-state and defend
the doctrine against all who fight it.

Often I have cried with the Psalmist, "My heart
is fixed, O God, my heart is fixed; I will sing and give
praise." Psalm 57: 7. "Surely he shall not be moved.
. . . He shall not be afraid of evil tidings; his heart is
fixed, trusting in the Lord." Psalm 112: 6, 7.

I know God called me to Christian work in early
childhood, at the age of nine. He kept me and trained
me in the school of faith, and, when the time was
ripe, He ordained that I should go and establish the
Kentucky Mountain Holiness Association for the
evangelization of the rural sections of the mountains
of Eastern Kentucky. The records of the past twenty-two years are telling mightly in the annals of
earth and heaven; thus proving that, "There hath
not failed one word of all His good promises which
He promised." I Kings 8: 56.

There is no doubt in my mind that God gave to
me the training, and threw around me those circumstances and educational advantages that have best
fitted me for this work of Faith to which He called

me in February, 1924 when I was a Senior at Asbury
College. When I entered Asbury, I had no other
thought but that I would continue with my evangelistic work all over the United States. It was a
bitter struggle for six weeks. But on the very day
I answered God's call for the rest of my life to be
spent in the Hills of Kentucky, indescribable joy and
peace swept over my soul.

I came in the strength of the Lord to this long-
neglected Home Mission Field, June 1, 1924. When
the tremendous conflicts and hardships came, as
they always do to test our faith, I could say, "The
Lord looked upon him, and said, Go in this thy might,
. . . have not I sent thee?" Judges 6: 14.

> *"The songsters in the arbour*
> *That stood beside the way*
> *Attracted his attention,*
> *Inviting his delay:*
> *His watchword being 'Onward'*
> *He stopped his ears and ran,*
> *Still shouting as he journeyed*
> *'Deliverance will come!'*
>
> *"I saw him in the evening;*
> *The sun was bending low;*
> *He'd overtopped the mountains,*
> *And reached the vale below;*
> *He saw the Golden City—*
> *His everlasting home,—*
> *And shouted loud, 'Hosanna!*
> *Deliverance will come!'*

> *"While gazing on that City,*
>   *Just o'er the narrow flood,*
> *A band of holy angels*
>   *Came from the throne of God;*
> *They bore him on their pinions*
>   *Safe o'er the dashing foam,*
> *And joined him in his triumph:*
>   *'Deliverance has come!'*

> *"I heard the song of triumph*
>   *They sang upon that shore,*
> *Saying, 'Jesus has redeemed us*
>   *To suffer nevermore!'*
> *Then, casting his eyes backward*
>   *On the race which he had run,*
> *He shouted loud, 'Hosanna!*
>   *Deliverance has come!' "*
> *"Then palms of victory, crowns of glory*
>   *Palms of victory I shall bear."*

When we give up all for Jesus and His Kingdom, the rewards are grand, and best of all we can glorify Him. While the blunders of my life have been many, yet this I say, "Praise God that He has helped me never to reserve anything from Him." The last atom of strength has gone into His work.

Like Caleb, "Forty years old was I when the Lord sent me to espy out the land. . . . Surely the land whereon thy feet have trodden shall be thine inheritance; because thou hast wholly followed the Lord." Josh. 14: 7, 9.

After twenty-two years of labor and trusting the

Lord for all things, I can truly say, as did Caleb, "I am strong this day as I was in the day that the Lord sent me: as my strength was then, even so is my strength now, for war, both to go out, and to come in." Josh. 14: 11. My soul doth magnify the Lord for all of His goodness and faithfulness to me. "He that loveth his life shall lose it; and he that hateth his life in this world shall keep it unto life eternal." John 12: 25.

Beloved, *faith is not an arbitrary gift of God,* but a faculty of the soul. Unless I had known by a real, tangible experience the saving grace of God, and thus been adopted into His family and then gone over into Canaan as a second definite work of grace, witnessed to by the abiding presence of the Holy Ghost in my heart, never could I have stood the tests or been given the strength to stand when the battles raged.

And now abideth faith, says the great apostle Paul. The abiding object of our faith is God and manifest in the flesh. Yes, the unchanging object of our faith is Jesus, both Lord and Christ. I fear that often the distinction between believing what God says, and knowing what God does, is ignored so that the real act of faith is omitted. This omission always produces a spiritless class of witnesses to regeneration and to sanctification. Just from theory they profess a spiritual experience which they do not possess. These dear souls are always powerless. They are devoid of love and often fanatical. They make light of the striving to "enter in" of others.

No doubt many dear people are innocent of their true condition. They have been taught "to take it by faith" and have no consciousness of any vital experience. They have been told—God says so, and I am believing His Word. The danger lies in the fact that they did not really get anything. You will hear them say, "I am standing by faith." Standing by faith, beloved, is neither the work of regeneration nor of holiness. These dear people have not received the "end of their faith." The end of one's faith is the salvation of the soul, and, if full salvation is sought, it is the actual cleansing of the heart from all carnality and the Holy Ghost coming in to abide. They have not *received* the end of their faith, they have only *believed* it. Receiving it is a conscious act. A reality to be received must be perceptible to the one that receives it. Of course faith in the truthfulness of God's Word is essential to any degree of salvation, but it alone is not sufficient for salvation. "Faithful is He that calleth you, who also will do it." I Thes. 5: 24. We must receive the thing His promise embraces.

This "believe you've got it and you have," has resulted in filling our churches and holiness camp meetings with unconverted and unsanctified people. It may be born of the idea to count numbers as success or it may be carelessness on the part of pastors, evangelists, or Christian workers that souls do not have a chance to get through truly to a heart-felt experience.

Let us *hold souls to a full surrender*. Thus God,

through the Holy Ghost will give them light on
what He require each seeker to do, whether con-
fessions, or making restitution, or whatever, in order to bring them into a vital relationship with Jesus
through His precious Blood.

"Therefore if any man be in Christ; he is a new
creature; old things are passed away, behold, all
things are become new." II Cor. 5:17. "The Spirit
itself beareth witness with our spirit, that we are the
children of God." Rom. 8:16. "Hereby know we
that we dwell in Him, and He in us, because He hath
given us of His Spirit." I pray that precious souls
who are seeking to be sanctified will be held to the
crucifying point of truly receiving. Often carnality
will dodge the issue, but the soul who really dies out
to everything, and lays all on the altar, gives his
whole will over to the Lord, and puts himself in a
place where he can have active, vital faith for the
cleansing Blood to be applied, will have indescribable rest of soul, rest from carnality with all its strife,
ill will, pride, and anger. I Cor. 3:3, "For ye are yet
carnal: for whereas there is among you envying, and
strife, and divisions, are ye not carnal, and walk as
men?" Jacob's faith worked when he confessed his
carnal traits (Gen. 32:27-29). When the disciples
became of one accord and tarried until their faith
gripped God, they were all filled with the Holy
Ghost (Acts 2:4).

"I am crucified with Christ: nevertheless I live;
yet not I, but Christ liveth in me; and the life which
I now live in the flesh I live by the faith of the Son of

Methodist Church — Honey Brook, Chester Co., Penn., where Miss McCornell was converted in January, 1898.

Poplar Grove School where Miss McConnell's M o t h e r taught before her marriage, and where the author and her three sisters attended school.

Central High School—Honey Brook Township where Miss McConnell was graduated in 1902.

God, who loved me, and gave himself for me." Gal.
2: 20. "For by one offering He hath perfected for
ever them that are sanctified. Whereof the Holy
Ghost also is a witness to us." Heb. 10: 14, 15.

*Many times meetings are hindered by spiritless,
inconsistent witnesses* who persistently profess what
they do not possess, in the place of standing by faith.
And thus they hinder the real work of the Holy
Ghost. This is one of the main causes that makes it
so hard to secure genuine conversions in our
churches, schools, and camp meetings. Beloved,
nothing can take the place of Holy Ghost unctionized
testifying, praying, and preaching.

An article in *The Pentecostal Herald* says of John
Wesley: "There was nothing stirring and gripping
in Wesley's ministry previous to his heart-warming
experience. There was nothing extraordinary about
it. There were no conversions under his preaching.
In describing his own condition he said: 'I dragged
on heavily.' He did his work through a sense of duty
without any spontaneous compulsion that fired his
heart from within.

"When Wesley received the conscious pardon of
sins and converting grace in that little meeting of
Aldersgate, he became one of the plainest preachers
of the way of salvation and one of its clearest teachers. The following expresses the thought:

"When a man has living faith in Christ then is he
justified. This is always given in a moment. And
in that moment he has peace with God, which he
cannot have without knowing that he has it. Being

born of God, he sinneth not." The article goes on
to say further:

"Wesley described the fruits of saving faith as deliverance from all uneasiness of mind, from the an-
guish of a wounded spirit, from all discontent, from
fear, and from sorrow of heart."

While the act of faith involves choice, it in itself
accomplishes nothing vitally spiritual. The act of
faith only makes it possible for the Holy Ghost to
accomplish His work.

So it was that with my heart full of faith and the
Holy Ghost, I came to the mountains of Kentucky
to help bring this blessed message of full salvation
to the isolated sections of the Hills. Soon after I
reached Breathitt County, I was told by one of the
doctors, a native of the County, and by one of the
lawyers that there were three thousand creeks in
Eastern Kentucky in the remote sections of the
branches, hollows, and ridges waiting yet for Sunday Schools and churches. The doctor said, "Miss
McConnell, there is an average of one a week killed
on the creek where I was born and reared." I knew
this condition could only exist because they had not
the Gospel of the Son of God. Some of the dear people in Jackson, and in the homes where I stayed
while holding revival meetings the first year, would
tell me about the fearful killings and happenings
along their creek until I thought my heart would
break for grief. I cried unto the Lord to give me a
ministry of love and divine power that would make
inroads on the enemy's territory. Year after year,

as souls have been changed from darkness to light, and entire communities made so different through the power of the gospel, my soul often says, "What hath God wrought?" "For a great door and effectual is opened unto me, and there are many adversaries." I Cor. 16: 9.

II

"THE MOUNTAINS SHALL BE THINE"

I was on my way to the Kentucky Annual Conference in the fall of 1924, where I was to be ordained a deacon by Bishop Theodore Henderson, of the Methodist Episcopal Church, when my heart became very heavy with the burden of the work. The enemy of souls was trying to discourage me. I took my Bible on that Chesapeake and Ohio train and began to read in the book of Joshua. God came with rich courage for me and spoke to me out of His Word. The verse, Joshua 17: 18: "But the mountain shall be thine; for it is a wood, and thou shalt cut it down: and the out-goings of it shall be thine: for thou shalt drive out the Canaanites, though they have iron chariots, and though they be strong," was quickened by the Holy Ghost to my heart. New joy, hope, and courage came over me so that my soul was lifted and the strength of this promise has never left me from that day to this. It was a rich token of His call. The task and vision of it overwhelms me yet.

I have been reminded many times while in prayer or at our conferences of one hundred and five pastors, teachers, evangelists, and helpers, of what the Lord showed to me when I was growing up on the farm back in Eastern Pennsylvania. *Many times I had visions* of having charge of a lot of people that were helping me in some work. I was telling them what to do and directing them in the various duties. That vision never left me. I told it to my sisters one time; they made fun of me. I never mentioned it again, but pondered it in my heart through the years. I often heard a voice say to me, "That is what you will be doing some day." When I was teaching school in Atlantic City, N. J., I would take special notice as to how the principal would manage the teachers and the eleven hundred students in our building, usually with the thought of my own future work in my mind.

After I had been in the work here for several years, I made known my former vision to my faculty. The Lord flooded my soul anew with His presence and said, "This is the fulfillment of the vision that I gave you back there." "And behold the glory of the Lord of Israel was there, according to the vision that I saw." Zech. 8:4.

When I said yes to God's call in my room at Asbury College, at once visions of churches and schools dotted all through the mountains came to me. I began to pray for the Lord to call others to help fulfill this vision. *Mrs. Mary Vandiver Swauger,* then a student at Asbury, came to me one day in March, 1924 and said with much emotion, "God has called me to the Kentucky Mountains." I was overjoyed to know that some day she would be there too. She came with me the first summer, but went back to college in the fall. She returned to the mountains in June, 1925. *She is therefore one of the pioneer workers and the first one called into the work.* God

has mightily used her to His glory. *I have asked her
to tell of the early days and beginning of the Mt.
Carmel High School and pastorates:*

"That Mt. Carmel Church and School was placed
in the particular spot it now occupies was no accident. The people in the community had a strong desire to have a church. A few of the people had found
the Lord in salvation, and were able to pray to the
end that someone would come to give them a church
where their children might be taught the right way.
What a touching thing it was to find a group of people with such hunger for the things of God. Can you
see them as they waited and prayed and planned to
try to build a church themselves? Then one day
three women rode up the creek announcing that
God had called them to build a church and school.
A thrill went through the community and soon meetings were being held to lay plans for getting started.
People came from other communities and the public
school teachers from three districts came bringing
their entire schools. With what eagerness and joy
the work began. The ground was cleared and the
foundations laid. None could doubt that God was
leading the way and selecting the spot for the hub
of the work. The doctrine preached then, and now,
was that of the Blood which cleanses from ALL sin.

"From this beginning of a church and a high
school, the work spread out along other creeks and
hillsides. In a few years church buildings were
erected where only the schoolhouses had been avail-

able in which to hold the services before. The pastors lived in such small houses as were loaned to them by the kind-hearted people in the various localities where the stations were placed. In those early days, the announcement of a revival was a signal for all to turn out night after night and souls prayed through by the scores. What a lift to the people of these communities to have Christian workers there to give them the light of the gospel after which their hearts were groping.

"As the years passed by, the power of the Lord continued upon the work. It grew, going deeper and wider. Seven counties are now included in the scope of its endeavors. Like the vine brought out of Egypt, the Lord 'caused it to take deep root and it filled the land.' 'The hills were covered with the shadow of it, and the boughs thereof were like the goodly cedars.' Psalm 80: 9, 10. But it was no longer ministering in the mountains only. A true holiness center is like a city set on a hill, it giveth light and that light cannot be hid. It was shining out into other states through the school and out into the mission fields through those going to foreign lands whom the Lord had called and sent through these halls to make their preparation.

"Thus from such a small beginning (the school and a few temporary stations), the work has grown to include a Bible School, and many stations with good church buildings and to cover territory in seven different mountain counties. Many of the mountain young people coming to these schools for training have God's call upon them to preach and to do evangelistic work. Some have also gone forth out of their own mountains to preach, as well as preaching at home. The Lord had done it all and made it all redound to His praise."

Yes, it was an outstanding event when the Lord gave Joshua 17:18 to us and thus He fulfilled this promise. Schools, churches, Sunday schools, camp meetings, missionary conventions, and conferences are all claiming the mountains. Step by step the Lord has helped us to follow Him and claim this promise.

Furthermore, while we are here on the field at the job for the Lord, He has raised up a host of *friends around the world who pray and give their support to the work*. Food, clothing, money and gifts have all contributed to the fulfillment of the promise. *The dear people here in the mountains* have done their share by giving land on which to build the churches and parsonages. Many times the community people where we build, will give lumber and also will help with the labor. Our hearts are always overjoyed when the burden of these material gifts is put upon the local people.

And best of all, *our precious converts* are helping to claim the promise of Joshua 17:18 by their lives and their prayers. It is through them that the gospel message grips the people and convicts them of their need of salvation. All the people love and believe the Bible. *There is no modernism here.* Thank God there is no battle along this line. If anyone would come into this country denying the Blood of Jesus as efficacious for sins, or scoffing at the Virgin birth, or telling the people that there is no heaven or hell, they would be driven out at the point of a gun. And I would say Amen to it. We pray much that only those will come into this needy home mission field who are true to God's Word.

On one occasion *a certain arch modernist from the East* said he was coming to Harlan County, Kentucky to preach to the people and settle a coal-mining dispute. Several people had been killed and he was coming to help their families. When I read this, I said, "No, brother, you had better not come or you too might have to look down a gun barrel. His message would not have been accepted by the community. The people are very discerning and they know sincerity and truth when they hear it.

Our work is very interesting because the people, who are true Americans and a home-loving people, have keen minds and open hearts. Our work takes us far back into the mountains as one woman in our stations said, "Away the tether side of yander." The native people farm the steep hillsides and here they raise their large families. In all parts of the world where there is much poverty, there is also great spiritual darkness. This is true in all the remote sections of the mountains of the Eastern part of the United States.

But the creeks, branches, hollows, and ridges are transformed by the converts. And "Tis the Old

Time Religion" that makes the change. And what a
glorious change it always is!

*A group of men were gathered on the porch of a
little country store.* One said, "This country is different." Another said, "Yes, not so much 'fittin.' "
Still another said, "Not so much 'killin'." Another
said, "Oh, them missionaries." Yes, it was the missionaries who brought the gospel message, but it was
the Lord who made the change in the hearts and
lives of the people. Praise God from whom all blessings flow. The gospel is the power of God unto salvation. "Therefore if any man be in Christ, he is a
new creature: old things are passed away; behold,
all things are become new." II Cor. 5: 17.

Here in our mountains the seekers pray through
in the old fashioned way. They come to the altar
night after night until they know their sins are all
forgiven and their hearts satisfied. Invariably, with
a glowing testimony, they will praise God for saving
them; then request prayer to go on and be sanctified.
It is this, dear friends, which makes the work very
encouraging and which glorifies God. A man, a
woman, or a young person whose carnal traits of ill-
will, hatred, revenge, and strife are all cleansed out,
makes a powerful impression on others of what salvation will do.

We had been here from June 1, 1924 until March
10, 1925 when we began the *building of the Mt.
Carmel High School.* God led clearly in each new
move that we made. Everything pointed to the carrying on of the full gospel message. We built the

High School for the sole purpose of reaching the
choice young people of the mountains. To have them
four years in an "A" grade high school under the
supervision of sanctified college men and women we
knew would be a big step toward getting the truth
before the people.

We were offered land in many places for the
school. After much prayer, we accepted the kind
offer of Mr. and Mrs. J. G. Lawson, although many
other offers were much better. However, when the
Lord gave us His extra peace and joy, we knew that
was His own leading and choice. We accepted the
lovely site of twelve acres, a beautiful, sloping hillside on the south bank of the North Fork of the Kentucky River in the northwest corner of Breathitt
County near Mill Creek. God has surely proved to
us ever since that this was the place of His own
choosing.

Through this school the Word of the Lord, these
past twenty-one years, has surely been published
throughout the mountains. Some years we have
*students come to us from sixteen counties of Ken-
tucky.* We pray much that the Lord will send us the
very students that He knows ought to be here. Consequently, we get a very splendid group each year.
Often, too many apply, but we trust the Lord to sift
them out.

At our commencement exercises in 1944 I was
giving a diploma to the youngest of a fine family of
eleven children. All of them had attended Mt.
Carmel School. They had walked over the moun-

tains and crossed the river two times each way and rarely ever missed a day. I said, "Daniel, what will Mt. Carmel do with no more of your family in our school?" He said, "Well, the grandchildren will soon be ready to come." Two of them are in Mt. Carmel this year, 1946.

There are scores of the Mt. Carmel High School graduates now teaching school and in other professions, besides those who are in full time Christian work. *The influence of the school is felt in every phase of life throughout Eastern Kentucky.*

In the two revivals each year and the regular Sunday preaching services, many souls prayed through and then became established in God's will and plan for their lives—a great source of blessing and encouragement to us. These young people are endowed with courage and power so that they are able to ask the blessing at the table and have prayer with their own families when they are home. This method the Lord uses to bring conviction to the people in the various communities. Some of the parents have found the Lord in their homes through the prayer and help of the young people.

It is here in the pliable years of high-school training that many find God's call for their lives to be given to Christian work. Two-thirds of the students that come to us have a call of God upon them. The majority are glad to say yes to the Lord, but some of them permit the enemy to sidetrack them. What a great grief to our hearts when they fail to fulfill God's will for their talented lives!

The Lord has certainly enabled us to produce a marvelous group of students who are a tremendous credit to the mountain country as teachers, business men, housewives, and Christian workers.

Many have gone on for three years further training in the Kentucky Mountain Bible Institute and are now in full-time service in their own "Native Hills" as pastors and as pastor's wives. God mightily uses them among their own people.

For the story of the building of the High School, I have asked one of my co-laborers who has been with the work for nearly twenty years, to write. R. L. Swauger was the first man to be called into the Kentucky Mountain Holiness Association. He came to us first to superintend the building and the next year God called him here. God answered prayer in sending us this capable man and God answered prayer while we built Mt. Carmel. He says:

"In the spring of 1925, just after the close of Asbury College commencement, eight young men left the campus and wended their way to the scene of their labors for the summer; the place that was later to be known as 'Baby Asbury.' It was located on a high hill above the North Fork of the Kentucky River, two miles below the mouth of Frozen Creek where it discharges its waters into the River.

"The eight young men were to erect the Administration Building on the campus of Mt. Carmel. After reaching the site of the building they established a camp, pitched an army squad tent for their living quarters, erected a temporary shed which served as kitchen and dining hall, and laid down a schedule of activities. The order of the day's work was as follows: Rising bell, 4: 00 A. M.; breakfast, at 4: 30, followed by family prayers and devotions; work beginning at 5: 30; dinner at 11: 30; with supper at 5: 30.

"The neighbors across the river would tell of hearing the songs of praise and the voices of prayer. Each boy had a chosen spot in the near-by woods for holding his own 'secret' devotions.

"All building material was shipped by freight from Jackson, the county seat of Breathitt County, to Frozen Creek. Here was a small siding where the carloads of building material were stopped. As already mentioned, the building was two miles from Frozen Creek, but the actual hauling distance was four miles each way with the river to ford once each way. It is worthy of special mention to note that during the entire summer, work of hauling was held up on only two days. The Lord favored the work in that marked way. In the years previous and in the years which followed, the river was very often unfordable. Such favorable weather sped the work much and to the Lord we give the praise and the glory.

"Since the weather was so ideal the boys were able to make splendid progress with the work. The building was a frame one, 67′x43′ with a full basement; the wall had already been laid before the boys arrived. Miss McConnell had made a contract with

a stone mason for $1500 to build the foundation. It
was finished May 10, 1925. All had a mind to work.
Much prayer was going up continually for the work
and the Lord answered. One of the men who helped
said he never saw things go together better, or saw
fewer mistakes made. God was aiding the carpenters surely. No accident of any account was suffered during the entire period. Underneath were
the everlasting arms. No harm shall come nigh
thee, was surely realized by each one as being a personal promise to him.

"In due time the building was under roof and
ready for the lath and plaster. Who was to do this
work? Six brothers, all lathers, came, set up a tent
and completed the lathing in a very satisfactory manner. Another answer to prayer. Now the plaster-
ing. A plasterer in Jackson was contacted but did
not give much promise of being able to take care of
the work. Yet in due time he came. God was undertaking.

"In connection with the hauling of the plaster an
event took place which is worthy of note. A car-
load of plaster had been placed on the switch at
Frozen Creek· The next morning eight teams were
ready to begin hauling. It looked like rain, but was
not raining. The plaster was needed. The drivers
were advised to start out, but to load up only on condition that the weather was favorable. Wet plaster
would be just so much lost plaster. Shortly after
the teams had left, the clouds lifted and the sun
shone brightly. All was well. Suddenly, one of

those quick hard showers came up. About fifteen or
twenty minutes downpour. Then all was clear.
What about the plaster? Ruined? Hardly. Within
about an hour after the shower all teams came in
with their loads as dry as could be. All the wagons
were unloaded. The last wagon was just leaving
the building where the plaster had been stored when
another hard downpour took place. It seems that
during the first shower, all eight wagons had found
shelter in our neighbor's barn, just across the river.
Before the second shower, they left the barn and
made the rest of the journey and unloaded. That
is divine timing. God is never too late or too early.
Such a remarkable event did not 'just happen'. This
work and all the material belonged to the Lord and
He was taking care of His material because we asked
Him to and trusted Him for it.

"All of the boys enjoyed the summer's work· It
was truly a time when it could be said, 'Here the atmosphere is pleasant.' There was no smoking, no
swearing, no foul talking. The carpenters were all
sanctified, working on a holiness church and school.
Instead of the oaths and cursings so often heard
around construction jobs, one might hear the strains
of 'Amazing Grace, How sweet the sound, That saved
a wretch like me,' or 'This is like heaven to me.' The
favorite song, however, was 'He's a Wonderful Saviour to Me.' It was sung with deep feeling because
it was true in each life. God's presence was on the
place. His help was evident in so many varied ways,
and His blessing was rich in the lives of the young

Mt. Carmel High School Campus

men. They could well say with Nehemiah, 'So builded we the . . . . . building.' "

———————

The Lord is near us and blesses us good in the work. Our many prayer meetings at the headquarters, which is the Mt. Carmel High School, are a mighty source of help. It is here where so many things need to be prayed through. Often we are melted down before the Lord in great gratitude for God's faithfulness to us. Here is what another of our life-called workers, *Genelle A. Day,* who has been with me nineteen years, and was the fourth to be called into the work, says about the seasons of prayer *Miss Day came into the work in answer to God's call in 1926. I have asked her to write about the Lord's help in our prayer seasons and also to give some of her pioneer experiences:*

"In fulfilling the God-given purpose of spreading Scriptural holiness in answer to God's definite call, one of the most potent means of gaining and keeping unity of mind and heart among the faculty members has been the regular faculty prayer meetings. Three times weekly we meet on a voluntary basis. The all-school prayer meeting meets each Wednesday night. Two times each week the young people meet for special prayer. We pray not only for our many needs spiritually and materially, but to have the borders of our own souls enlarged.

"God has signally honored this means of grace and has quickened our hearts time and again with gracious promises and assurance as we have united in

prayer before the throne. Especially have the
prayers of Miss McConnell brought God near in the
out-pouring of His Spirit in a mighty canopy of Shekinah glory. We are urged to make our supplica-
tions with much praise and thanksgiving, thus dis-
pelling the darkness of any oppression of the enemy
and bringing glory to Jesus.

"In one of these prayer meetings in the early years
of the work, there swept from heaven upon each of
us a mighty vision of the working of the Holy Ghost
in our midst. God showed us the headquarters of
the Kentucky Mountain Holiness Association in a
leaping, blazing flame of spiritual fire. The hills and
valleys loomed before us, and out from this central
fire we saw little fires catching here and there until
the whole hill country was aglow with a mighty con-
flagration of spiritual warmth and blessing. To these
fires were coming the cold, darkened, sin-benighted
souls for the light of salvation. The glory and blessing of this gracious revelation has inspired our hearts
time and again when the fruit of our labors in some
places was hidden for a season.

"With this end in view we have gone forth to pray
and labor and love souls, through revivals in the
little schoolhouses or in our own churches built in
answer to prayer. The fires have been catching now
these many years so that today, scattered among the
hills, are many hearts warmed and blessed by the
Holy Ghost as they minister to their own people in
their own home and from behind the pulpit."

The outstation pastorates have claimed the ful-

fillment of Joshua 17: 18 through these years. Our
pastors who live in these sections ride horseback
or walk thousands of miles each year. Where there
is a road good enough to travel on through most of
the year, some few have cars.

On one occasion three of our pastors were making
calls. They had visited and prayed in many homes
that day. They kept asking if anyone lived farther
up the creek. So they went on from home to home.
Finally, they had gone so far that they were getting
a bit weary. However, they were told there was one
home yet, away at the head of the hollow. They
walked about two miles farther and found a dear
little lone mother only nineteen years old with three
children. She was so happy to see them that she
cried for joy. She said she had not seen anyone
for two years except her husband. After some time
the missionaries said, "Could we have prayer?" She
said, "No, talk to me." They stayed until her little
heart was happy. Then she said, "Now you can
pray." They reached their little parsonage after
dark, but felt blessed and happy after the good day
of telling the folk about Jesus.

"I have heard their groanings." Acts 7: 34. We
find throughout the many communities where we
have places of worship that people have prayed
for someone to come and tell them about salvation.
Here is a sample of thousands of those hidden away
in the fastness of the mountains who are hungry to
find the Lord. One of our pastors tells the following
incident:

"What a blessing it is when one finds some old
sanctified saints who, in spite of age and feebleness
extreme, still have the joy of the Lord in their hearts.
In an isolated place not far from our pastorate is
such an example. Years ago, before Mt. Carmel was
founded, this dear saint read in the Pentecostal Herald of Miss McConnell and her hopes and aspirations
for the hills. She was so impressed that she sent her
an offering to her address in Jackson, Breathitt
County, where she was living that first year. This
woman's experience of holiness is still bright and
clear and she enjoys telling how she obtained the
blessing. She tells it in a way that warms one's soul.

"At this time she lived two and a half miles from
her county seat town. She had listened to the conversation of two holiness preachers as to how persistent they had been in seeking the experience. So,
for many nights in succession she arose from her bed
while everyone was asleep and prayed that she too
might be entirely sanctified. One night after what
seemed to be another fruitless effort, she retired and
just then it happened. Her suppressionist husband
was asleep and after a futile attempt to remain quiet,
she awoke him to tell of the blessing she had received.
He was so impressed that he was led into the experience. He has since gone on, but some of these days
she will join him again and they will doubtless remember that night when God satisfied her heart's
desire and cleansed her heart."

For years we prayed for evangelists to come and
help us. God gave us a very remarkable lift when

He began to call our own mountain young people who had been trained in our schools to the work of evangelism. God said to one of our girls, "Do the work of an evangelist." She was the first to be called to this very important phase of the work. Later the Lord laid His hands upon three of our men, then on two of our women. Now, with our three schools and many outstation revivals it keeps them busy.

———

Our grade school at the Lee City station has done a very outstanding work. The two teachers and the two pastors there feel greatly rewarded because of the spiritual and educational results. Furthermore, through this school the community is helped spiritually. *A product of this school writes:*

"I have been privileged to attend a Christian school ever since I started in school. In the little Mission School at Lee City, Kentucky, which is a branch of the Mt. Carmel High School, you could always feel the blessing of the Lord.

"The Lord has dealt with me ever since I can remember, and my heart was tender. He first saved me when I was but seven years old. I well remember getting down at the altar and confessing out my sins. I didn't know very much about salvation, but I knew enough to understand that we had to be saved and sanctified before we could get to heaven, and I surely didn't want to be left behind. After my conversion, my mother got under conviction to know the Lord too. She would tell me night after night when I

would come home from school how she had been
praying that day for the Lord to save her, and finally
one day the Lord came in and saved her, and that
was a big answer to prayer for just a little seven year
old child. I do praise the Lord for it.

"In the seventh grade I heard a voice speaking
to me. I didn't know what it all meant then, but I
am thankful there was no rebellion in my heart toward His will. That voice was saying, 'I want you
to preach here in the mountains for me.' I was so
startled I hardly knew what to make of it or whether
it was just my own idea because my father and
mother had said they wished their children could
be out in missionary work.

"For a few days I didn't know whether to tell of
God's call or not for fear I might be mistaken; but
one day I finally managed to get words together
enough to tell mother and then I told the pastors of
the church. There was so much blessing when I
told it that I didn't know whether I was still here on
earth or had changed worlds. From then on I could
not doubt the calling of the Lord.

"One day in the Mission School, the Lord gave
me a chance to talk in chapel. I was nervous because
that was a big task for a timid little girl, but the Lord
gave me a message from the book of Acts. It told
of the time when Felix was almost persuaded to mind
the Lord. It was during the revival services at school,
and I felt that some of those boys and girls were almost persuaded to mind the Lord, too. I was so
happy to see a number of my schoolmates get saved

that morning. How it did encourage my heart!
I shall never forget that blessed service.

"After my grade school days the Lord led me on
to Mt. Carmel High School. Circumstances were
against my coming here, but He gave me many good
promises. One was, 'I will lead thee by thy right
hand, saying unto thee, Fear not I will help thee.'
Finances would be impossible I thought because I
did not know where everything was coming from.
My father wasn't able to pay my way. But then the
promise came, 'Seek ye first the kingdom of God and
His righteousness, and all these things shall be added
unto you.' I could not doubt the Lord any longer
and so I came on; and I have been surprised at the
way the Lord has answered my prayer and has supplied my every need and even more than I need.

"I am sorry that I did not always keep true, but
I praise the Lord that, after wandering around in
the wilderness and eating on the husks of sin as it
were, the Lord did save and later He sanctified my
soul, and I know it was real down in my heart. I
praise Him that He can save the deepest sinner if
we really want His will.

"I long to see the time when I can really be out
answering the call the Lord gave me back in my
grade school days. That early call grows dearer to
my soul every day. Winning souls for Jesus is going
to be worth more than all the things we could ever
get out of sin. I praise Him that He has put a love
in my heart for my own people and I don't want
them to miss heaven just because I haven't done my

part, but I want to be faithful to them always, and finally merit my Lord's 'well done'."

———

Our *Kentucky Mountain Bible Institute* was started in 1931 in Breathitt County in a large old commissary building which was given to us. We repaired it at a cost of $1300. Then we built a dormitory for boys at a cost of $3500. When we had been running the school for only eight years, a Flash Flood washed it all away. But God rebuilt it, in answer to prayer. The new location is three miles from the old site on land donated by a kind neighbor man, Mr. Fred Fletcher. The new location is also one mile from the Mt. Carmel High School.

Again God's leadings were manifest in that He knew this phase of the work would help to get the gospel to the mountains to fulfill the promise of Joshua 17:18. This excellent three year's course beyond their high school training for those called to Christian service is a source of firm establishment to the young people. For three years here they study the Bible, Theology, Church History, Greek, English, Homiletics, Vocal and Instrumental Music, and kindred subjects.

During their years of study here, each student is also assigned to an *outstation pastorate*. This pastoral work affords an excellent practical foundation of training for the work of the Lord. Here is fulfilled II Tim. 2:15: "Study to shew thyself approved unto God, a workman that needeth not to be ashamed, rightly dividing the word of truth." Also,

II Tim. 3: 17: "That the man of God may be perfect, throughly furnished unto all good works."

In our Kentucky Mountain Bible Institute the power of the Holy Ghost is mightily manifested upon the faculty and students. God uses our Institute not only for training the young people whom He has called into the mountains, but also to train scores of others whom God has called to foreign lands to spread Scriptural holiness. Some are already working for Him there now.

The account which follows telling of a dream of one of our Mt. Carmel High School girls truly fulfills the objective of our labors:

"God at sundry times and in divers manners has soon fit to speak to people in a manner that is not ordinary. Bunyan said he dreamed, Peter and Paul said they had a vision, Daniel said he had a dream and visions of his head upon his bed.

"I awakened one night and found God speaking to me. In those days when vacation time came at Mt. Carmel we students could either walk twelve miles across the country, or four miles in another direction to the highway and pay twenty-five cents to ride the bus sixteen miles and then walk four miles on home. We usually found it easier to walk twelve miles and pay nothing, than to walk eight and pay the twenty-five cents; because those were depression days. Always, after a week-end at home and the long hard trip back to school, as we would come over a hill into sight of Mt. Carmel the place

looked almost like heaven to us. In fact, it was a
little world within itself·

"Thus I went to bed and dreamed I was just coming over the hill into sight of Mt. Carmel. I could
feel again that I was about to reach my desired
haven when the angel of God came over to meet me
and talked with me. (Please keep in mind that I
was only a high school Sophomore). The angel
said, 'Do you know there is more to Mt. Carmel than
that which you see with your eyes?' That startled
me because I thought Mt. Carmel was the prettiest
place in this countryside, but I lifted my eyes to look
again upon the place when I saw just the opposite
of what John saw about the New Jerusalem. Instead
of coming down from God out of heaven, God was
there on that hill-top and a great shekinah glory
rested over Mt. Carmel in the form of a great building that extended into the heavens. Then, suddenly
we were inside the building viewing the Christian
students. The angel of God called my attention to
the halo of glory or God's great presence that rested
over each person who was living for Jesus and 'doing with his might what his hands found to do.'
Maybe God permitted me to see that because I was
a work student. I saw those who cooked during the
summer months, those who worked on the new
buildings on the campus, while some had been sent
out to stations. The angel of the Lord called my attention to the gracious presence of God that rested
upon them. Immediately we too, were the same.
Really it was like the Millennium, and I have since

found that God's sanctified people enjoy a great rest and an abiding sense of His presence comparable to the Millennium. 'There remaineth therefore a rest to the people of God.' Heb. 4: 9.

"Again the scene changed and we were in the chapel. There was an altar that extended all the way across the front end of the building and all the way down one side in the shape of a great 'L'. All the front end wall of the chapel was gone, thus making one big door. All rivers, hills, and every obstruction was gone and in their places ran a great highway which we all understood reached to every nation. People of every nationality passed over this road, some in cars, some on horses and mules, multitudes walking, as so many do here in our mountain country. Then I noticed a great altar service was in progress. People of every sort were seeking and finding God. The teachers or faculty members of the Association were stationed every so far apart all up and down this altar to instruct those who came and to help them pray through to victory. Untiringly, they exhorted the seekers and helped them to God.

"Miss McConnell stood on the raised platform and painstakingly watched the people as they passed. The Christian students stood in a group waiting for her to tell them who should go out and bring in the people from off this great highway whereon all nations were traveling. We watched carefully. We stood always on our feet ready to do as we were bidden and looked right at her. Suddenly, she would

see someone, and without a word would point to one
of us and then point to a certain person on the road.
We walked straight to the road and told the person
to come in and seek Jesus. All up and down that
roadside were students bringing people to that great
altar where all the faculty stood stationed to help
them through. I vividly remember one of us bringing a colored woman off that road to find Jesus. She
hitched her horse under the tree and was brought
to the altar where stood a faculty member from
the South. She knelt in front of the colored woman
and helped her to Jesus. The woman stood up, testified as to how her sins had been washed away; then
went out, got on her horse and rode away.

"This bringing in of souls went on for sometime.
Then Miss McConnell saw a soul in drastic need
about to be lost forever. He was dressed like a Hindu
and was barefooted, riding an ass and carrying
the casket of a child in his lap, as I had so often seen
happen on Devil's Creek where I lived. We students saw his distress and all looked at Miss Mc-
Connell, hoping to be sent to him, for we knew
whichever one she sent could bring him in. We all
understood if he got past us he would be lost forever. We all became exceedingly moved upon. Miss
McConnell looked at one student after another,
pointed to them as they were ready to run, and
shook her head. At last she pointed to me. How I
wanted to run! She shook her head as we all became white faced. And the soul was lost forever.
Because someone had failed to answer God's call

and hence was absent in the time of greatest need.

"I awakened, changed position in bed and thought, 'My! what a nightmare!' After sometime, I fell asleep again only to go through that same altar scene from beginning to end. But the second time I witnessed the awful scene of that soul dropping into an endless hell. I awakened, got on my knees there by my little cot in my high school room and sobbed and sobbed and prayed and prayed, asking God to help me to be so submissive to His will I would always be ready to be sent wherever He saw I was needed and that no soul would slip into hell because I couldn't be found on the job when needed. For days I cried over what I had seen. Then I would get blessed as I thought how those numbers came to Jesus.

"One day I was having my devotions aloud. When I finished and came out of the room, a teacher said, 'Child, are you burdened or blessed?' I said, 'I don't know.' I feared to tell lest I be considered strange, but one thing I did know and that was that my head and heart were set to answer the call to minister to my own native people which God had given me over on Devil's Creek before I ever heard of Mt. Carmel or calls. On that night back on Devil's Creek when I had prayed through alone at the age of seventeen, one thing I promised God was that if He would save me, whenever I got a chance to go to the store or post office or to the mill, I would tell souls everywhere that they really could be delivered from sin. Soon missionaries came to our creek and told us of Mt. Carmel. Later, I had the privilege of finishing at that school and then of completing the course at our Kentucky Mountain Bible Institute.

"More than nine years have passed since I finished Bible School, married, and have been in missionary work. God's rich blessings, guidance, and help are more abundantly upon my husband and me each day."

God has raised up a great host of prayer partners and friends who support our work. This, beloved, is a mighty factor toward claiming the fulfillment of Joshua 17:18. Your rewards, Dear Helpers, are piling up both there and in heaven. "Lay not up for yourselves treasures upon earth, where moth and rust doth corrupt, and where thieves break through and steal: But lay up for yourselves treasures in heaven, where neither moth nor rust doth corrupt, and where thieves do not break through nor steal." Matt. 6: 19, 20.

The Mountain Missionary Society of Asbury College has been a great source of help and encouragement to the work from the very beginning. Their regular weekly prayer meetings have helped lift many of our burdens both spiritually and financially. The spiritually-minded young people also interest students so that through these years dozens of the young men and women of the College have come to help us in the schools and pastorates. Some stay for a few years while training for the foreign field; others have answered God's call for their lives here. God bless Asbury and reward her continually for her splendid and far-reaching contribution toward the spread of Scriptural holiness over these Hills.

The following is an account of one of our revivals. It is written by one of our mountain girls who spent seven years in our school and is now a pastor. This, beloved, is the rapid fulfillment of Joshua 17:18.

"Week after week the faithful Christians were meeting together for prayer services on Wednesday nights and Sunday mornings. The main burden of these prayers was for a revival. Every soul was crying out against the powers of evil over the unsaved and their sins individually. Not only were the Christians of this one mission praying thus, but faithful people all over the mountains in our Association, and in other states too, were united with us. Our cry was, 'Lord, send us an evangelist full of the Holy Ghost and faith. Send us a revival of true soul-saving and sanctifying power. Destroy the works of the devil in this place. Save souls at any cost. Put the enemy clear out of the community.'

"God had blessed His promises to our hearts. 'Did not I say unto thee, that if ye believe ye shall see the glory of God.' To another, 'Ye have not chosen me, but I have chosen you and ordained you, that ye should go and bring forth fruit and that your fruit should remain.' John 15:16. Outward circumstances were dark and absolutely unpromising. Yet,

in every heart there was perfect assurance from the
Lord that He was working and that we were going
to see the glory of God through the salvation of
precious souls.

"On May 6, 1945 the revival began. God had sent
the evangelist full of the Holy Ghost and faith; and
He also sent us a lady with the same qualifications
to play the accordion and lead the singing. Every
sermon was just what we needed. The glory began
to fall right away. The first soul victory came at 2: 00
P. M. prayer meeting. At the close of the prayer
service two hungry-hearted women were invited to
the altar and one truly was converted. Old fashioned
shouting began right there. This was the first prayer
meeting she had ever attended, but never has she
been sorry to this day. Soon she went on into holiness and is enjoying the blessing of a sanctified heart.

"We had prepared ourselves to continue in revival effort until we should see the desires of our
hearts if we had to keep at it all summer. However,
God took complete charge of everything and everybody and at the end of two weeks we felt free to
close. A number had prayed through to glorious
victory. The altar services were wonderful. A
young woman wanted her parents to get saved,
though unsaved herself. One night she led the way
to the altar and began praying out of a burdened
heart. Her father fell by her side and began business with God. A number of burdened souls were
lined up at the altar, every one really seeking salvation or sanctification. The father of this young

Kentucky Mountain Bible Institute Among the Hills

woman soon got saved. Someone started to say a word of encouragement to the girl and she said, 'I'm already saved, but I want God to save Daddy too.' He was sitting on the altar, face all aglow. Then she was told that he was saved too. She jumped up, threw her arms around his neck and said, 'Daddy, I'm so glad you've got God.' He testified later that he went home that night in the dark, went to his coat pocket, got his tobacco, and threw it away. Later they were both sanctified, and two happier souls were never seen.

"A number of others, men, women, and children likewise got gloriously saved and sanctified. They quit their tobacco, drinking, cursings, and all sins, and began real life in the true way.

"Instead of hearing God's name being taken in vain, and quarreling, it was the greatest delight of our hearts to hear family prayers ring out over the valley and that old hymn, 'Amazing Grace,' truly come from the heart's depths of those who had experienced this change. 'Take the whole world, but give me Jesus' became our theme song.

"After our conference at Mt. Carmel, the same evangelist went to another station about twenty miles away to hold a revival. We were so glad it was summer, for night after night this group of redeemed souls, and some who wanted God, gathered from all over the community to a truck which took us to this revival. As we went over the road to and from the services these twenty miles, our hearts were so full and blessed that we sang many old

hymns as we rode along. The words rang out into
the air in such a spirit that people all over the country knew that we had experienced a genuine revival.
Praise God from whom all blessings flow.

"Those who were convicted deeply went along to
the meeting and continued to go to seek the Lord in
this revival until they found victory. The words of
that old song, 'It is truly wonderful what the Lord
hath done,' just expresses how we felt as we stood
back and watched God work."

---

*The work of the Kentucky Mountain Holiness As-
sociation has extended so far that we now have it
divided into four districts, North, South, East, and
West. In the center stand Mt. Carmel Church and
School, the headquarters of the work.*

In May, 1945, the pastor of one of our stations in
the South District and his wife sent for me to come
over. It seems that one of the men along the Creek
wanted to donate land to the K.M.H.A. on which to
build a church and parsonage. We drove as far as
we could in the car. Then the pastor met us, and we
all walked from there, climbing two very steep
mountains. Then we followed a creek bed, either
jumping or wading across as best we could in many
places. Just at noon we reached the house where
the missionaries lived. The pastor's wife served us
a fine dinner.

We then went to this gentleman's home to draw
up the deed. We talked it over and all was satisfactory; he could give us a clear title to the land.

We then went to see the land—a three-cornered piece on a hillside. After we had stood there a while, planning where to put the buildings, we had prayer. We poured out our hearts to God in thanksgiving, and then and there we dedicated the ground on which we plan to build one more lighthouse for the salvation of the people in that far-back community of Breathitt County. The gentleman who was giving the land, and his wife and others were present. As I said, "Thank you Mr. ——." I saw that he was crying. "I wouldn't be surprised," I said to him, "to hear that you will be one of the first to get saved and sanctified in the new church. God bless you. I'm praying for you."

God has extended the work far back into the mountains so that we now have *twenty-eight places of worship*. In many of these places we have our own church and parsonage buildings. When we dedicate the new churches what a time of rejoicing we have because of one more lighthouse on a long-neglected creek or ridge.

God surely has been glorified when someone has given money to *build a church in memory of a loved one*. This month, March 1946, I received a letter from a dear friend saying she wanted to build a church in memory of her husband who had gone on to be with Jesus. I wrote her that the cost is $1500. Most of the labor is donated and sometimes some of the lumber, hence the small cost. I often tell the Lord that we are gladly giving our lives here without a salary and somebody somewhere must be raised up to build our churches and parsonages and pay our many bills. I know it pleases the Lord when a group of people or an individual contributes largely toward a new church in a community where there never has been a church or Sunday School. I say without the shadow of a doubt that folk are laying up treasures in heaven when they help us to carry on in this soul-saving center where many Blood-washed saints are enjoying heart-felt religion as a result of this work of God's own planting.

"Bring ye all the tithes into the storehouse, that there may be meat in mine house, and prove me now herewith, saith the Lord of hosts, if I will not open you the windows of heaven, and pour you out a blessing, that there shall not be room enough to receive it."

When I started to live by faith, some folks told me that I would starve and others said some very discouraging things. I have needed very little money. In fact, I have, on the average, spent less than sixty dollars a year on myself during these past twenty-two years. The Lord has taken such good care of me. He has blest me with excellent health these last ten years. He has raised up friends all over the nation. My soul is refreshed in this Canaan Land warfare more and more each year. As the burdens and responsibilities pile up, the Lord has taught me to cast all my care upon Him and take my burdens to Him and leave them there.

Our work fulfills the promise of Acts 1:8, "But ye shall receive power, after that the Holy Ghost is come upon you: and ye shall be witnesses unto me both in Jerusalem, and in all Judea, and in Samaria, and unto the uttermost part of the earth." *The word "both" means Home and Foreign missions* that God intends should be carried on at the same time. "Both in Jerusalem and unto the uttermost parts of the earth." God has led us to do this very thing, not only the mountains, but also in the region beyond. "The outgoings of it shall be thine." Josh. 17:18. *The testimonies that follow have been received from some of our young people who, in recent years, have gone out from here to lands across the sea.*

"The memory of the good prayer meetings, chapel services, revivals, and constant careful teaching, blesses my heart and I thank God again and again that it was one of 'the good' things that He wanted me to have. God surely dwells on Mt. Carmel.

"During my third year the Lord definitely called me to Africa. The Holy Spirit sealed the call to my heart by a rich outpouring of joyful blessing. I knew from then on that Africa was my place. The early knowledge of His will helped me in many ways to hold steady and to know better what I wanted in school. I always like to remember the covenant I made with the Lord in my youth.

"After finishing four years at the high school, I went to Bible School at K.M.B.I. Besides studying and learning some things from books I am glad for the practical training in going out with others on Sundays to preach and teach Jesus. I am also thankful that I learned to work with my hands. That is a very definite part in training to be a missionary. We were taught to cooperate and make adjustments. Today I praise God for the wonderful privilege that has been mine. I shall ever remember the sacred place and the lessons taught. Truly His glory covers the entire work."

"Although I am not a Kentuckian, I feel that the benefits I have received and the debt I owe to the work of the Kentucky Mountain Holiness Association are as profound as that of many of those for whom the work was started. I am tremendously grateful for the providence of God which led me there, for the spiritual blessings I received, and for the lessons I learned. I count them among the most valuable preparation I received for the mission field.

"I went with a Christian experience which had grown cool in college through years of careless living, but honestly wanting better things. Although I went as a stranger, I recognized at once the genuineness of their religion and the presence of God in the place. Their message of the heart-cleansing Baptism with the Holy Spirit, a second definite work of grace, was unanswerably presented from the Word and evidenced in the lives of the workers. I feel quite confident that if all Christians could openheartedly and without prejudice hear this doctrine Scripturally presented, and see it lived in the lives of those professing it, that few, if any, would remain unconvinced of its truth.

"I spent one year at the Kentucky Mountain Bible Institute. I was convinced at once of the truth of their message and later of my own need. In the K.M.B.I. chapel I retook the ground I had lost in my years of careless living and again was conscious of the witness of the Holy Spirit that I was His child and the past was graciously forgiven.

"I rejoiced in that victory. My heart was hungry for the Second Blessing. The next day I asked Mr. Swauger if he would pray with me and we went to my room and prayed. I gave myself to Jesus, all I was, and ever hoped to be, and meant it. I died to self and sin, and asked for a clean heart and the infilling with the Holy Spirit. I struggled with faith a little and then accepted the Blessing. I thank God for that experience and the Holy Spirit that came to abide. I have kept Him, and He has kept me from then until now. He gives me rest of soul and peace continually. He has delivered me from fear of people, and adds His presence and blessing to my efforts to preach His Word in a way I had never previously known.

"I am deeply grateful for the help I have received from Miss McConnell and the other workers in the K.M.H.A. I count them among my most valued friends and am proud to be considered a product of their work.

"I rejoice also to see, in this land among our colored brethren, that this same message of Full Salvation works in its mighty transforming power, and the power of God can, and does, take black folk with a heritage of centuries of ignorance and superstition, and save them from their sins and baptize them with the Holy Ghost. We have seen it and are seeing it. Praise God!

"The Lord is blessing us good here at Mutaho and we are seeing a goodly number seeking the Lord every Sunday for which we are very thankful. Getting our Christians sanctified is a harder pull, but some are getting the Blessing and others seeking it. What we need is a Pentecost. Pray for us. We send our love and prayers and best wishes to you all."

"I shall always be thankful to God for bringing me to India via Kentucky. In the spiritual atmosphere at Mt. Carmel my soul become established in holiness. During this my first year in India, I have again and again praised the Lord that while in Kentucky He started teaching me how to get the leadership of the Holy Spirit. We learn best by experience. To train young teachers they are given classes to teach under the supervision of experienced teachers. Thus to be trained for Christian work, one must do the work. In the Kentucky Mountain Holiness Association young workers are enabled to do a real soul saving work under godly, experienced leaders. In the spiritual battle for lost souls we learn some of Satan's tactics. We have seen God work! Going from there to the mission field we go confident that our God can defeat the powers of sin and darkness.

"Today I rejoice in the fact of a heart made clean by the Blood of Jesus and the abiding presence of the Holy Ghost. Without Him, as a missionary, I could do nothing. How often this past year with the many problems which daily confront one this verse has proved true, 'The Holy Ghost shall teach you in the same hour what ye ought to say.' Holiness, I find, works well in India."

"There are a number of reasons why I am deeply grateful for the five and one-half years which I spent in the K.M.H.A. before coming to the mission field. First of all, it was at Mt. Carmel in an atmosphere of prayer and godliness that I came to realize the sinful condition of my heart. It was there that I found pardon from all my guilty past and freedom from inbred sin through the cleansing of the Holy Ghost. I am also thankful for the excellent training, mental as well as spiritual, which I received both at Mt. Carmel and at the Bible School, under the ministry of consecrated, Spirit-filled teachers.

"Not only that, but by close association with many sanctified teachers, workers, and students I learned that people from different parts of the country and from different churches, people with different personalities and different backgrounds, and with different likes and dislikes can live together in perfect harmony if they are thoroughly saved and sanctified. To me, this has been a great source of blessing and encouragement ever since I left the warm fireside of the K.M.H.A. In looking back over the years spent there I say with the Psalmist, Truly, 'The lines are fallen unto me in pleasant places; yea, I have a goodly heritage.' "

A splendid boy whose parents were born and raised in Kentucky tells about God's call:

"I came to Mt. Carmel in 1939. The flood occurred about three months before. My mother brought me here, but it was the Holy Spirit that spoke to me, and I knew it was the place for me. I was professing when I came, but when I saw the other students happy and able to go to bed without a worried look on their faces, I began to want the same thing. In fact, when I came on the campus, I felt a pull toward heaven. I had been there about two weeks or so when I felt that I was the meanest old sinner that ever lived. I had covered the fact up long enough. I headed for the altar and that is where God gave me real joy.

"The following day the Lord sanctified me. The experience of sanctification was not as I had previously thought of it. I found it was an actual experience that made a change in me. The carnal heart that was so unlike God was gone. In its place was the blessed Holy Spirit. I was then fifteen years old. It has been real throughout the years.

"During my first year at Mt. Carmel, in one of the boys' prayer meetings in the administration building, the Lord spoke to me and asked me if I would go to Africa. My heart was so blessed to think that God called even me that I wanted to shout, but still I wanted to know for sure that it was God. Before the prayer meeting was over, all doubts were gone. In the seven years since then some things have bothered me, but one thing has always been settled

—my call to Africa. I was anxious to help others to find Christ. Many times I took the chance to pray with the ones that I roomed with in the dormitory. I was glad, too, for every opportunity to speak in the chapel services or in any other services.

"Ever since I received my call I knew that the Lord could not use any but a willing worker. I tried to do my best in everything I did. Many times, as I realize now, I failed to do my best, but God helped me. I did not have the money to go to school without working. My people were not able to pay my expenses; so the next thing for me to do was to trust God. This trusting has brought some of the greatest blessings I have received. God has never failed. He saw me through my high school and Bible School days. I worked all I could and stayed on through the summer time and worked, not merely for the money I would get, but for the practical experience. When I could help on the buildings and get a chance to preach, I felt I was helping someone else who was going out to help the lost world.

"In 1945 the Lord led me to Asbury College and has been taking care of my every need. He has never failed me. As I look forward to Africa, I have no fear. The Lord has called. He has led me thus far and I am sure that a thing as little as the ocean cannot hinder the working of our God.

"Mr. Swauger has meant much to me. The times that he has talked and prayed with me, I can never forget. Mt. Carmel has meant more than words can tell. I will always feel indebted to that dear

place. The six years I spent there will mean much
—all that I learned there in books and practical
work, in preaching, building, and farming—will be
invaluable to me when I get to Africa."

---

*One of the adjoining counties to Breathitt has sent
us many splendid young people. One of these girls
writes of her call to a foreign field:*

"As far back as I can remember there have been
missionaries on Devil's Creek where I had the privilege of attending Sunday School and church. My
mother was sanctified in the early days of the work
there. I have always lived in the atmosphere of a
Christian home and have grown up around a family
altar. Miss Margaret Thompson was one of the first
missionaries to Devil's Creek. I did not know at the
time that she was praying for the Lord to call some
young people of that creek to Africa. The Lord answered prayer and gave three of us a call to this field.

"I have always had a longing in my heart for the
things of God. I came to Mt. Carmel when I was
fourteen, as an Eighth Grade student. It was during my first year at Mt. Carmel that the Lord laid
His hand upon my life for Africa. One night after
I had gone to bed, I could see a group of colored boys
and girls out in front of me, and the Lord told me
that that was where He wanted me. For several
months I never told anyone about it, until one day
my brother was talking to me about calls. He asked
me if I ever felt that I had a call. Then I told him
about the Lord's dealings with me. He encouraged

me to mind the Lord and answer the call. I have never felt any rebellion in my heart against God's will for me. It was God-given and I love it. I have only one aim and desire in life and that is to let my life be burned out for Him in Africa.

"When I came to the place of complete surrender to the whole will of God, and died out to everything, friends, loved ones, and future ambitions, the carnal nature was taken out and the Holy Ghost came in to abide, and now I am enjoying two definite works of grace in my heart.

"The Lord gave me five good years at Mt. Carmel, and then led me to Bible School for three years of further training. Here I can get established in holiness to go out for Him as a missionary to Africa."

A Morgan County boy, with a God-given call upon him, writes:

"On September 7, 1938 I was led by the hand of the Lord to Mt. Carmel High School. I was a hungry-hearted boy who had been fighting conviction for several years. The sanctified lives of my parents and the good preaching in my home church, which is one of the Association outstation churches, made life miserable for an unsaved boy. When I came to Mt. Carmel, conviction deepened and life grew more miserable because of the load of sin I was carrying.

"I was first saved in the fall revival at the school. My sins were all forgiven and my life was really changed. When I went to the altar, they did not tell me to believe, but told me to confess my sins to God.

When I had confessed everything that came to my
mind and I knew that all of my sins were gone, then
I was ready to believe. When I believed God the
change was made. That experience was good, but
I knew from my past teachings that there was another step to be taken.

"I had heard the doctrine of sanctification as a
second work of grace since I was a small child. My
next step was to get that blessing which made me
clean from the pricniple of sin, 'the old man' as Paul
calls it in Romans. Now I had a bright outlook on
life. The past was all under the Blood and I had
really started living.

"When I was a Sophomore in high school, the Lord
spoke plainly to my heart and told me that He wanted
me to be a missionary in Africa.. I said, 'Yes, Lord,'
and have been planning to answer that call ever
since. I have had four good years of high school
and three better years of Bible School and expect to
spend my best years serving the Lord in Africa.
Praise His name!"

---

*One of our young women who is on her way to
India writes:*
" 'God works in a mysterious way His wonders
to perform.' It was no accident that my brother
from South Carolina attended a camp meeting in
Findlay, Ohio on the same day that Miss McConnell
had part in a missionary service there. God looked
down and saw this young man along with his brothers and sisters. He knew that in this family were

laborers for the Home Field and also for the Foreign
Field. He saw that they would need preparation for
their life work. He knew where they should get
that training. Thus He arranged the events of that
day.

"That was our first introduction to the K. M. H. A.
In that same year God called me to be a missionary
to India. At that time I was completing my studies
in a Junior College. Shortly after graduation, my
brothers suggested that I join them in the Kentucky
Mountains. Knowing that God was leading, I came
on December 27, 1939. Almost four years have
been spent in the work since that time. These years
have been of inestimable value to me. My experience as station worker, student, and teacher have
drawn me closer to God and developed my Christian character. While in Bible School I learned
much about the Bible and Theology, but the lessons
in practical Christian living hold the preeminence.
I rejoice that God led me into a place where I could
see and recognize His workings.

"I know that the lessons learned while there will
stand me in good stead wherever God leads me. I
have already had many opportunities to prove Him
faithful while away from the work, completing my
degree and teaching in a public school. After receiving my A. B. degree in the North, I came to teach
at Mt. Carmel. I have received innumerable blessings here. Last year I taught in a public school that
paid me a good salary. Then I came to a place where
there was no salary. Most folks cannot realize that

the joy and peace found in helping young people to walk with God is far greater than material wealth. This year has truly been the happiest of my life.

"In the last two months the way for me to go to India has opened. I know that this opportunity has come about because I have minded God and kept in His will by working in this needy field; for it was through this Association that I contacted the mission board under whom I am to work. All of this has been brought about by prayers of Christian friends. Again, I thank God for Christians who not only pray a call upon young people, but continue those prayers until the young people are actually answering that call."

———————

The president of the Kentucky Prayer Bands writes as follows:

"A secret of power and blessing in the Kentucky Mountain Holiness Association is that throughout every phase of the work there is a great concern— that of spreading Scriptural holiness around the world as well as at home. In our camp meetings and conferences, our vision has been increased through the years under the ministry of such missionary warriors as Dr. and Mrs. C. W. Troxel, Rev. and Mrs. Woodford Taylor, Dr. and Mrs. G. Arnold Hodgin, Dr. John C. Wengatz, Miss D. Willia Caffray, and many others. Good missionary books are included in our conference course of study each six months. Although closely associated with the National Holiness Missionary Society, we are interested in every channel for getting the full salvation message to heathen lands.

"In every one of our outstations we have a missionary prayer band which meets regularly for the purpose of learning the burdens of the foreign field and praying definitely for them. Each new outstation means additional prayer bands. As revivals are held in these places and souls get saved and sanctified, new recruits are also added. The Christians early learn to carry the burden for souls beyond the seas. Many of these sanctified men and women are now leaders in their own communities in advancing the cause of foreign missions. As a result, some of their sons and daughters have heard the call to the foreign field. A number of our outstations have been blessed with the privilege of entertaining the Kentucky State Prayer Band Convention.

"Praying and giving go hand in hand. The faith with which these people have pledged to give what seemed nearly the impossible, only to reach the goal and increase the amount each year, is marvelous to behold. The amount given adds up to several thousand dollars over a period of a few years. This money is given with sacrifice, and out of deep gratitude because the full salvation message reached their own hearts, so delivering their hearts from sin, that they are eager for those in heathen darkness to know this message also. Children, as well as many unsaved men and women, have opportunity to hear and share through the medium of our Sunday Schools. One Sunday each month is set aside for

perhaps the telling of a missionary story during the
opening exercises. The collection on that day is
given for missions and is considerably larger.

"Visiting missionary speakers, prayer band meetings, nights of prayer, and similar activities make our
schools centers for foreign missions. The majority
of students in our schools have definite calls. Esther
Faulkner, a choice mountain girl, became burdened
that someone in Mt. Carmel might be called to India.
The answer to that prayer was a definite call that
she herself should go. She rejoiced in being a part
of the tithe sent out from the mountains to the re-
gions beyond. She is now fulfilling that call in India, after having completed several years of holiness
training in our schools. Already a number of our
Bible School graduates are on the field and several
expect to go soon. The future ministry of those
called to the home field is enriched, and the burden
for foreign missions is increased through having
been in these missionary centers. Even the boys
and girls in our Grade School love missionary stories,
give generously of what they have, and pray for
other boys and girls in the mission schools of other
lands. God has His hand on some of these very
young lives.

"Young men and women from our Holiness Bible
Schools and Colleges find the home mission field of
the K. M. H. A. an invaluable training ground for
preparation before going to the foreign field. Lessons in praying through obstacles, in living by faith,
and in holding on until victory comes are most valu-

able to any missionary candidate. In our outstation work, or in teaching in the schools, circumstances continually present themselves which, by God's grace, develop one's tenderness, understanding, and patience. These God-given opportunities demand greater responsibility to faithfully live and preach holiness and deliverance from all sin, to those who still wait in heathen darkness.

"Praise God for the great part the Kentucky Mountain Holiness Association is having in spreading Scriptural holiness over this poor needy world."

III

FAITH—MIGHTY ANSWERS TO PRAYER

"Jesus Christ the same yesterday, and today, and forever." Hebrews 13: 8. There is no need for one to enlarge upon present-day conditions throughout the world, and especially since World War II.

I quote from President Truman's speech given at the Federal Council of Churches meeting in Columbus, Ohio on March 6, 1946. "The last five years have produced many awesome discoveries in material things, but it has been truthfully said that the greatest discoveries of the future will be in the realm of the spiritual. There is no problem on this earth tough enough to withstand the flame of a genuine revival of religious faith.

"If the civilized world is long to survive the gigantic power which man has acquired through atomic energy, it must be matched by spiritual strength of greater magnitude.

"The church has a supreme opportunity now to fulfill its mission on earth," he said, and added, "We must provide the shock forces to accomplish this moral and spiritual awakening. No other agency can do it. Unless it is done, we are headed for the disaster we deserve. Oh, for an Isaiah or a St. Paul to reawaken a sick world to its moral responsibilities. Present world conditions call for a moral and spiritual awakening in the life of the individual and

in the councils of the world." What a challenge to
every church and every member!

The solution is found in Psalm 50: 14, 15: "Offer
unto God thanksgiving; and pay thy vows unto the
most High; And call upon me in the day of trouble:
I will deliver thee, and thou shalt glorify me." Mal.
3: 7: "Return unto me, and I will return unto you,
saith the Lord of hosts." Nothing is impossible with
God. "For this God is our God for ever and ever:
he will be our guide even unto death." Psalm 48: 14.

We are hidden away in the Hills of Kentucky
where God delights to answer prayer. The *aroma of
answered prayers* is constantly with us. We find no
other explanation to our faith than that God is and
that "He is the Rewarder of them that diligently
seek Him." Heb. 11: 6. Like Paul, we too can say:
"I count all things but loss for the excellency of the
knowledge of Christ Jesus, my Lord." Phil. 3: 8.

Our lives have been enriched because each new
extremity has been a fresh opportunity to prove
the inexhaustible resources of God. Praise His dear
name! He has been more than equal to every emer-
gency.

Psalm 32: 2: "My soul shall make her boast in
the Lord: the humble shall hear thereof, and be
glad." Verses 8 and 9, "O taste and see that the Lord
is good: blessed is the man that trusteth in Him.
O fear the Lord, ye his saints: for there is no want to
them that fear Him."

In January, 1945 about ten A. M., while school
was in session, we looked toward the boys' dormi-

tory and saw smoke coming from every window and
from under the roof of the entire building. It was
evident that the building was on fire, and the fire
had gained much headway. At once the classes
were notified. The boys and men teachers rushed
to the building, gathering up fire extinguishers as
they went. The girls and lady teachers followed
with water in whatever vessels they could find. We
directed them to get water from the fish pond and
not to bother with the electric pump or the cisterns.
At once the men and boys began to tear the boards
off the walls so as to get at the fire in between the
partitions. Others carried all the furniture out of
the entire building. We kept up a constant proces-
sion carrying water. No one showed excitement.
All worked with marvelous poise. After all direc-
tions were given, I went to the office, not to watch
the fire, but to pray while all the others worked. In
less than ten minutes I had the assurance that the
Lord heard my petitions. In one-half hour the fire
was all extinguished. God answered our heart cries.
"They called upon the Lord and He answered them."
Psalm 99: 6. God knew that we had no water system, and no insurance, and that it was in the middle
of the school year.

We met in the office at once for a season of praise
to the Lord for sparing the building. The way the
fire had started was: One of the Senior boys had
been drying his overalls on a line above the open
gas stove in his room. The line broke. Of course the
clothes caught fire and burned a hole in the floor.

This set the room below on fire. Two rooms burned and some of the lower floor hall. Only God could stop such a fearful blaze. All through the day we thanked the Lord for this definite answer to prayer.

Mr. Swauger figured out the needed materials that same afternoon, and went to Lexington in the truck to get the lumber. The Bible School boys and Mr. Fisher, one of the professors there, together with our boys and faculty began the work at once. Mr. Fred Fletcher, a kind neighbor, Mr. Glen Taulbee, one of our fine converts, and one of our outstation pastors came to help also. In less than a week it was all repaired. The boys doubled up four in a room and thus we got along quite well. Everyone had a mind to work. God is so good to us and we never cease to give Him all the glory for His great care and overruling providences.

Soon after school opened in the fall of 1945, we had *difficulty with the discipline problems* as we so often do at the beginning of each new school year. Some of the boys were giving trouble. My soul was so burdened, I could not sleep. We held on to God in prayer and faith until God gave us the assurance that the devil's power was broken. Things cleared up, and our hearts rejoiced over the marvelous victory of the Lord upon us. "Greater is he that is in you, than he that is in the world." I John 4:4. Jesus is stronger than the devil. He knew how to rout the enemy off our campus when we trusted the Lord fully. One stanza of Charles Wesley's hymn expresses our victory at that time:

"The world with sin and Satan
In vain our march opposes
Through Thee we shall
Break through them all;
And sing the song of Moses."

One of my dear friends who had known me all my life kept telling me that she had remembered me in her will with $1000. I would see her at least once a year. She would tell me of her gift. She became almost helpless during the last eighteen months of her life. This necessitated getting a nurse. An R. N. and her mother came to take care of my friend. Toward the close of her life she was at the mercy of these two women who were no kin to her or even friends in any way. They succeeded in changing her will almost entirely in their favor, and were very careful to see that none of her dear life-long friends should see her alone.

This meant that her money did not go where she had wished it to go. Many of her close friends and some relatives were keenly disappointed. Some wanted to contest the will. I was notified to come and get some furniture that she had given to me, but was informed that no money for me was mentioned in the will. The Lord so quickly lifted me out of the disappointment and grief of it all. He comforted my heart and let me know that He would make it up to us and lift our many burdens some other way.

Two of our fine mountain boys and I made the trip for the furniture in the truck. We planned services

in churches both going and coming. The round trip
was about two thousand miles. On our way there,
we held a service in a Methodist church in central
Pennsylvania. A dear saint of God said to me, "I
feel led to give you some money to help in your work
to build a church." I am giving you $1500." I said
at once that the Lord had laid this on her heart when
I was so tenderly lifted by God's rich comfort, at the
time of the fearful disappointment at not getting the
long-promised $1000 from my dear friend. God
knows how to do the "exceeding, abundantly, above
all things" for us. Our gracious Lord takes care of
the interests of His kingdom. "And it shall come to
pass, when he crieth unto me, that I will hear, for I
am gracious." Exodus 22: 29.

Early in December, 1945, our *food bills* had
amounted up to $1665.87. (They are more than
$10,000 each year). When they get above $800.00
we surely become concerned. Sometimes I say to
the wholesale house manager, "Our bill is getting
very high." Invariably he will say, "We have no
worry about it. We know what you have done."
This time it was burdening me much. I tossed on my
bed one night. I could not sleep; the burden was
too heavy. All at once, the Lord said to me, "I'll attend to it." "Thy prayer is heard." Acts 10: 31. I
fell asleep right away. In less than two weeks we
paid $800.00 on it. In three weeks it was all paid.
However, the next day it was up again to nearly
$300.00. It takes a lot of food to feed a hundred and
fifteen people in our two boarding schools; but I be-

lieve that in this way, as we pay our debts, faithfully, we are spreading Scriptural holiness.

Mr. B—— of the wholesale house in Jackson, Breathitt County, told us that the head man of the company a few years ago was inspecting the books. He came to our account which was then over $900.00. He said to Mr. B——. "What about this account? It is too large. Who are these people?" Mr. B—— explained that we were missionaries running two boarding schools and doing it by faith. This scared the man worse. He said, "You had better see to it, and watch this account." Mr. B—— said, "I'm not a bit afraid because I know these people and what they have already done." The president of the company came back in less than a month. He said, "How about that account of the Mt. Carmel School?" It was all paid. The man was much astonished. What are we doing? Proving to the people that the Lord answers prayer. In this way we have many opportunities to show the goodness of God to those who walk with Him in this holy way.

Some of the men in the Kiwanis Club in Jackson have said to me, "Miss McConnell, we sometimes talk about you in our meetings." I said, "What do you say about us?" They said, "We think it is a miracle how you pay your debts. We marvel at your faith." I told them it is because the Lord has given us clean hearts through the cleansing Blood of Jesus when He sanctified us wholly. Thus the hindrances to faith are removed. "And hereby we know that we are of the truth, and shall assure our hearts before him. For if our heart condemn us, God is greater than our heart, and knoweth all things. Beloved, if our heart condemn us not, then have we confidence toward God. And whatsoever we ask, we receive of him, because we keep his commandments, and do those things that are pleasing in his sight." I John 3: 19-22.

In the early years of the work two of us felt led to pray about a certain very trying problem. A bootlegger was selling liquor to our students and to the folk who came to the services at Mt. Carmel. We had no consultation with each other but God laid this heavy burden on us. Finally, we said to each other, "I am definitely asking the Lord to handle this fearful situation." In less than six months the man moved out of the country many miles away. When we truly put things in God's hands, He loves to take care of every circumstance. "Commit thy way unto the Lord: trust also in Him; and he shall bring it to pass." Psalm 37: 5. We praise God that on June 10, 1946, Breathitt County was voted dry by a good majority of 1077.

Sometimes we hear how the Lord is using our trust in Him to convince the people in our field of labor that the Lord is so powerfully on our side through the many answers to prayer. The gentleman who helped us clean out an old gas well near our Kentucky Mountain Bible Institute on Frozen Creek in 1934, was in a country store where a number of men were gathered. One man said, "I don't believe that God answers prayer like He used to in

Bible times." Our friend spoke up and told the crowd
about his experience with us concerning the gas
well. "God gave gas to those folk in direct answer
to prayer," he said. "I was there when it happened."
He went on to relate the entire incident.

We praise God for these *miraculous things that
bring glory to Jesus* and conviction for salvation
upon the people. The Lord caused the earth to open
and give His people gas. He who made the earth
and knows all about it loves to help His people when
they ask unselfishly and for the advancement of His
kingdom. "Where wast thou when I laid the foundations of the earth? declare, if thou hast understanding." Job 38: 4. He laid the foundations of the earth,
just as He caused the tempest to cease and the sea
to become calm and the sun to stand still. "And he
arose, and rebuked the wind, and said unto the sea,
Peace, be still. And the wind ceased, and there was
a great calm." Mark 4: 39. "Then spake Joshua to
the Lord in the day when the Lord delivered up the
Amorites before the children of Israel, Sun, stand
thou still upon Gibeon; and thou, Moon, in the valley
of Ajalon. And the sun stood still, and the moon
stayed, until the people had avenged themselves
upon their enemies." Josh. 10: 12-14.

We needed more gas on our Mt. Carmel High
School campus. We were getting gas that was escaping from an old well that had been plugged up. The
supply from this well which was twelve hundred
feet off the campus was now very inadequate, because we had more buildings. We felt that the Lord

would have us drill another well. We prayed and discussed it together many times. Finally, the Lord gave us the assurance that the time had come for us to proceed to drill.

We secured a man from Ashland, Kentucky. Mr. Guy Meabon and his son from Huntington, West Virginia, so kindly helped us move the big gas well drilling rig to the campus. Now the rigs are very large and weigh tons and tons. We ferried it across the Kentucky River near the mouth of Frozen Creek on trucks. Then we made an improvised road two miles up over the ridge and down to the campus.

We asked the driller to set up the rig on a certain spot about three hundred feet from the boys' dormitory and about the same distance from one of the girls' dormitories. He said, "No, let us set up over here on this little knoll because it is easier to set it up here and easier to drill. You will strike gas anywhere in this part of Breathitt County." We said, "We are praying to get gas six hundred feet down. (Brother Meabon, the sanctified man who helped us move the rig, is an old gas well man. He said, "I believe if we pray, God will give us gas at six hundred feet in big lime strata of the earth.") This struck a note of praise in our hearts, because it takes great faith for an undertaking like this with all the other financial burdens of the work. The cost was to be two dollars per foot, but the driller was very kind and said that because we were in Christian work he would drill for $1.50 per foot. We were most grateful for this. However, when I told him that we felt the rig should be set up in a certain spot because we were praying to get gas at six hundred feet and that this was the place where we felt it should be drilled, he said, "To please you, I'll set it up right where you want it." He laughed much at the idea of praying for gas to be found only six hundred feet down. He said, "I have been drilling gas wells in Eastern Kentucky and in West Virginia for thirty-five years, and I never struck gas above fifteen hundred or two thousand feet in this part of Kentucky." We went on praying and the men kept on drilling day after day.

My, how the enemy did try to discourage us. The big stem, weighing two thousand pounds and twenty feet long was crooked and thus the hole became crooked. It was a powerful job to get it straightened out. The stem would stick every time. The driller said, "We will have to start another hole. We will never be able to get this one straight." We said, "No, we feel the Lord has shown to us that this is the very spot where the well is to be drilled."

Mr. Swauger, one of our professors, managed to get this big crooked tool over the Kentucky River by winching it across. Then he loaded it onto our one and a half ton Chevy truck and took it to Allen, Kentucky, eighty miles away. The shop there straightened it . The welding bill was $125.00 The hole was soon straightened. That battle was won by the help of the Lord. I tell you faith and works go together. It takes both to prove God's will and to please Him.

The next thing the big walking beam broke. This too tried our faith, but again we trusted the Lord, and fitted in another walking beam. The driller himself was not there nearly all the time. He had hired some men from Ashland, Kentucky, to do the work. They got discouraged and quit. Mr. Keeneth Grantier, a good sanctified man and one of our neighbors, helped much. He had moved into the Lawson community from Pennsylvania to educate his children in our Mt. Carmel High School. He had done much drilling of gas wells in Western Pennsylvania. He was truly a God-send and a great encouragement to us. He helped with the work and prayed and advised with us. George Thomas, a Quaker boy from Oregon who was with us to get practical training before going to Africa, also helped with much of the work. He was very faithful to the work of drilling, and also prayed hard. The Lord surely wove into his young heart and life much faith which he is now using to the glory of God in Africa. The mutual burdens and fellowship in prayer over this one big undertaking were a great source of blessing to all of us.

To our grief the next accident that happened was the breaking of the sampson post. It was a tremendous big thing at the top of the rig. Well, again Mr. Swauger was given wisdom to get it replaced with a new one. We started the work of drilling again. The Lord was on our side and kept us encouraged. "If God be for us who can be against us."

We kept drilling and praying. The second day of

July, 1942, we heard a great sound like steam escaping. We rushed from every building on the campus to the site of the gas well. The men were standing back, their faces and clothes all splattered with white clay. They had struck gas. You could hear the sound of gas escaping for at least a mile up and down the river. We asked, "How far down are you; how deep is the hole?" They said, "We just measured it before we put the stem down the last time. It is five hundred and eighty feet deep." That was twenty feet above our faith! We fell on our knees and praised God for one more miraculous answer to prayer. That day we had three prayer and praise meetings.

We wired the driller at Ashland to come at once. He came the same day expecting that we had just struck some little pocket of gas. He was amazed. We told him that the Lord had answered prayer. God gave us a well of 500,000 cubic feet of gas with two hundred and ten pounds pressure. It is going strong today after four years of constant use for heating, cooking, and power purposes.

We were three days trying to tie it in. The three hundred feet of six-inch casing would bob up and down in the well because the pressure of the gas was so great. Finally, we made heavy three-foot iron braces and bars and thus got it tied in. The driller said if we could have sold the gas that escaped those three days it would have amounted to $2100. We did not want the gas for selling or for making money. God knew our unselfish prayer and thus He answered. We had prayed all the time, "Oh God, don't let us strike oil, we might get rich and backslide."

George Thomas slept by the well for three nights lest someone might light the gas. We knew there was no way to put it out if it ever got on fire; the flow was so powerful and fierce as it roared out of the six-inch hole only five hundred and eighty feet deep.

We needed to have the gas harnessed so as to run the furnace in the main building. We had been burning coal for the past seventeen years. We wrote to various companies about a janitrol (these are instruments made to control gas that goes into the furnace to regulate the heat). The price was $495 each, beside the freight and the cost of installing. Mr. Swauger began to pray and ask God to give us a plan. The Lord showed him just how to make a burner of two-inch pipes, and one-inch pipes, and elbows and trees, and to use the Bunson Burner plan. He set it up and it has worked perfectly all these years. The cost was exactly twenty-one dollars. We praise God for another definite answer to prayer. "But seek ye first the kingdom of God, and his righteousness; and all these things shall be added unto you." We apply this promise often in this work of faith.

One day a neighbor lady sent a note to us by one of her sons. The note read: "Do you want to buy our *farm?* We are moving away. I need hospital treatment." We prayed about it. All felt led to go and see if we could buy it for a reasonable price. The farmer asked $8000 for one hundred acres, most of which was hillside land. (When you buy farms in the mountains you always pay for more acres than you get. You only get about seventy-nine or eighty acres and pay for a hundred). We did not even consider it at that price. He sent for us again. We did not go. We discussed it from every angle and as we prayed we felt that the Lord wanted us to buy it. We offered a price which we felt was very fair. The house was very good, but needed lots of repairs. The barn was not so good. They said they would not sell it for that price. We dropped the matter by saying that we felt that was all it was worth. They sent for us the next day saying we could have it for our price which was $4500.

A lawyer had said, "Wait awhile and you will get it for two thousand dollars less. The man is so deeply in debt he will soon be sold out at a sheriff-sale." We said, "No, we don't do business that way. We want to pay just what the place is worth."

I went to the bank and said to the president, "Will you let us have some money? We have bought Mr. S——'s farm." He asked us how much we wanted. I replied, "$4500." He answered, "Yes indeed." I put my name to the note, and said, "Mr. T——, we will pay this back in a year." "I know you will," he answered. God sent us money through kind friends from all over the country. Many paid for one or more acres. It was all paid for in less than a year.

We praise God for this good lift toward helping us with our food supply. While the land is poor, yet it affords pasture for our Jersey cows and helps with the garden vegetables. And best of all it is helping our young people to get an education by working on the farm to help pay their expenses.

"Blessed are they which do hunger and thirst after righteousness: for they shall be filled." Matt. 5:6. Surely the Lord knows how to guide hearts that are hungry and do not have the Light. Sometimes we find precious souls whom the Lord so tenderly led into a real heart experience, even though there was no one to tell them the way of salvation. Water Baptism cannot save us from our sins; it takes the Blood of Jesus. Thank God for the hunger that is implanted in every heart. "As the heart panteth after the water brooks, so panteth my soul after thee, O God." Psalm 42:1.

The following testimony of our dear Mrs. Blanche Haddox proves God's love for hungry souls who want to know the Lord in all of His fullness. She was one who helped to pray us into her neighborhood.

"I am so glad to give my testimony because of the heart-felt and know-so facts about the matter. From the very early dawn of my life, I wanted to be saved and be a true child of God. I certainly didn't want a maybe-so or a guess-so case. I wanted it in reality, in all of its fullness. Thank God, I did get it that way.

"When a little girl of eleven years of age I joined the church and was baptized. I was in earnest and

that was the best I knew to do then. That was my
first step toward the kingdom.

After I was married I found myself questioning
and wondering if I were truly saved and fit to die
should death come. Then, I thought, as a professing
Christian, was I all God wanted me to be, living with
an unsaved husband, and having three little innocent children in my care. Oh, if I should fail to be a
helpmeet to them to find the way of life as God had
laid it down for us all. The thought was troubling
me and one day at the close of a revival meeting, I
got hold of a gospel tract and the headlines were,
'Are you converted?' Well, that got me and I was
very troubled about the matter for I knew I was not.
I had no heart change, no joy, no testimony only that
I had joined the church and been baptised.

"I started praying and trusting God to regenerate
my heart and give me the witness in its fullness of
truth that I was His child through the Blood of Jesus.
I had no help except the Holy Spirit, but I kept on
praying and reading God's Word almost day and
night, searching for a promise. One day He gave me
the promise in Matthew 7:7 that blessed my heart
much: 'Ask, and it shall be given you; seek, and ye
shall find; knock, and it shall be opened unto you.'
Well, that is what I continued to do, till one night
about eleven o'clock He really did come in. Bless
His dear name. He lifted the awful burden of sin
off of my heart and gave me such peace and joy and
I surely could know of a truth the work was done.
My heart was regenerated and I was a new creature

in Christ Jesus. Oh, dear hearts, I am so glad He can do the work truly. You will never need to question or worry about it again.

"It was not very long until I saw and felt I had another need. I noticed things in my acts and deeds sometimes that I felt were not Christlike; He was not pleased with my conduct, and my temper would rise up now and then in spite of all I could do. I had never heard anyone speak of a second blessing nor had I ever read anything in regard to it, but I began to seek and inquire of God, asking Him to deliver me from all the ugly things I could see in my life. I had no help or information from anyone, whatever. Some told me to stop seeking that I would lose my mind for I was a good woman, and living a good life, and that I would be saved anyway, but that did not discourage me a bit. I did believe with all my heart that God could and would meet my soul's need as I tried to describe it to Him. Bless His dear precious name, one day about ten o'clock, after I had a good season of prayer, He surely met my soul in a marvelous way. I never shall forget it. Waves of peace and joy flooded my soul. I could know of a truth the work was done. I was so happy; I rejoiced in Him. I could go around telling others about it, though I did not know what to call it only that I got a second blessing from the Lord, and that there was greater power and blessing than I could describe.

"Not until I saw our dear Miss McConnell the first time in my life and heard her testify to it, did I know what to call it—sanctification. I said to myself as she explained the way of holiness, 'That's just what I have got.' I do so praise and thank God for the witness of it in my own heart. It is blessed to know that anyone can have it that wants it. Amen! Praise His name forever!"

IV

"SO MIGHTILY GREW THE WORD OF GOD AND PREVAILED"

All of our *revival meetings* are times of great soul travail for our pastors, evangelists, Christians, and the entire Association. In the spirit of faith and prayer we enter into each one fully expecting to see things come to pass in the advancement of the kingdom of God. Furthermore, the revivals are hailed with great joy and much praise. We depend fully upon the Lord through the preaching of His Word to release Holy Ghost power on the community.

Our Spirit-filled pastors and evangelists do all in their power to promote revivals and then to help the converts to get established. This takes much self-denial and minding the checks of the Spirit. They pray much and fast in order to better carry out the apostolic injunction, "Take heed therefore unto yourselves, and to all the flock, over the which the Holy Ghost hath made you overseers, to feed the church of God, which He hath purchased with His own blood." Acts 20: 28.

We do our best to turn the meeting over to the Lord and then ask Him to direct us. We know it is real faith when we turn over to another to do for us what we cannot do for ourselves. Hence, God gives us marvelous demonstrations of His divine Power. The secret of any of our success in soul-winning in

the mountain country is due to the fact that we
strongly emphasize the need of Scriptural holiness.
"For I have not shunned to declare unto you all the
counsel of God." Acts 20: 27.

Our workers do not reserve anything from God.
Their last ounce of strength is used for the promotion
of the work of salvation whether in revivals, visitation, teaching, building of churches, pastoral work,
or whatever it may be. They live in the spirit of holiness and their hearts are all ablaze with the fire of
the Holy Ghost.

The marvelous harmony that prevails among our
large group of workers (representing twenty-two
states and twenty-three denominations) is not because we require high standards of qualifications
scholastically, but because there is one common center of attraction which is enjoyed by everyone, that
of a clean heart. To be well oiled by the Holy Ghost
takes out the things that hinder the smooth running
of any organization.

We have learned to rely upon the divine forces,
not to overpersuade or coerce. We do not look at circumstances or stubborn wills, but keep on looking to
Jesus and the power of the Holy Ghost to break
down every barrier. Commissioner Brengle said,
"The Lord save us from planning our meetings so
that the Holy Ghost does not have a chance to work."

These Christian workers have all been made free
from sin in their souls through the sanctifying power
of the Blood of Jesus, and endued with Holy Ghost
power. "... But tarry ye ... until ye be endued with

power from on high." Luke 24: 29. "Sanctified, and meet for the Master's use." II Tim. 2: 21.

Not only in revivals do folk get saved and sanctified, but God gives us lovely hand-picked fruit in our schools and stations in our regular services, and in our pastoral visits. The pastors also do the work of an evangelist, as Paul commanded Timothy who had charge of the churches. The pastor is called not to preach only, but is called to *save souls* by preaching. The entire ambition of the pastors of the Kentucky Mountains Holiness Association is to win souls. God has truly given them the passion for the saving of the unsaved.

Here is the testimony of one of our evangelists whom God has raised up in our midst and trained in our schools.

" 'O Lord, revive thy work in the midst of the years.' Hab. 3: 2. Revivals have always been of special interest to me. At the age of sixteen years I was gloriously converted in a revival meeting. As soon as I was converted there was a desire in my heart to work for the Lord. I felt I would like to be an evangelist, but kept all this to myself for I had little or no thought at that time that Evangelism would ever be my calling.

"On February 3, 1930 God unmistakably led me to Mt. Carmel High School. A revival was in progress at the time I arrived. The young people were getting saved and sanctified and also some were getting their calls settled; some to foreign fields and some to preach in the homeland. I had been at Mt. Carmel only three days when the Lord definitely called me to preach. My call was sealed with a great manifestation of joy and blessing on my heart and on those who were around. I have never been able to doubt my call from that day till this.

"As time went on it became a growing conviction that the Lord was calling me in the words of Paul to Timothy, 'Do the work of an evangelist.' Even though that was the very thing I had always desired to do, when I faced the reality of it, and began to see what it really meant, I was not able to say 'yes' without a struggle. My delay in going into the field of evangelism resulted in many heartaches. However, since cutting the shore lines and launching out into full-time evangelism, there has been much joy in witnessing God's dealings with others and seeing them pray through. So much good has come to my own personal Christian experience through my full-time evangelistic work that I regret deeply my reluctance to take the step several years sooner. My advice to others whom God has called shall always be: 'Obey, promptly and thoroughly.'

"During these years in the Lord's work I have had many, many answers to prayer that have rejoiced my heart.

"My first revival was held in one of our mountain stations. The promise God gave me as I was on my knees was Isaiah 41: 15, 'Behold, I will make thee a new sharp threshing instrument having teeth; thou shalt thresh the mountains, and beat them small, and shalt make the hills as chaff.' This revival was attended with much blessing; likewise, with stiff opposition. Night after night the young men of the community would disturb and try to break up the service. They would throw rocks on the roof and against the house. One night while I was preaching, a good-sized, lighted fire-cracker came through the window and fell on the pulpit by me. I brushed it off and went on preaching. One night some gun powder was rolled up in a paper and laid in the window and a match struck to it. We all thought at first it was dynamite, but were relieved to find out it was not. The Lord helped us to go on with the service. My parents, who lived only a few miles away, would ride horseback over the rough roads night after night to attend the service and make sure that no harm should come to me personally. One of my first cousins likewise came for miles almost every night for my protection, though that reason was unknown to me until later.

"In spite of all the opposition of the enemy, God honored our faithfulness and answered our prayers and gave us souls. One night I didn't get to preach at all. The blessing of the Lord fell and souls lined the altar, so that the entire time was turned into an altar service. Such earnest seeking of the Lord I can never forget. Truly we can say with Paul, 'Nay, in all these things we are more than conquerors through Him that loved us.' Rom. 8:37.

"God has led us in all our revivals to place great emphasis on Scriptural holiness as a second definite

work of grace, an experience for every believer,
meanwhile not failing to put due emphasis on the
other doctrines and truths of the Bible. We see gracious results in lives here and there. Always when
the believers get sanctified, the power and blessing
of the Lord is released as a result of their walking
in the light so that sinners are convicted of their
sins and made hungry for salvation.

"In one of our revivals a lady was a faithful at-
tendant at every service. She had tried at different
times to live the Christian life, but had failed as often
as she tried, because she had never been instructed
as to how to get rid of the carnal nature. One Sunday morning she was reclaimed and shouted and
shouted. In a short time, when the altar call was
made for believers to get sanctified as well as for sinners to get saved, she came without any hesitancy
and prayed through to a glorious experience the very
first time she sought for heart purity. More than
twelve years have passed since then but she is still
rejoicing in this 'Grace wherein we stand.' The whole
community in which she lives regards her as a holy
woman.

"In lots of cases our revivals take us back into the
communities where the students from our High
School and Bible School live. Their consistent Christian lives leave a good impression on their families,
relatives, and neighbors and they are able to pray
through largely as a result of the lives of these students. We found one mother deeply under conviction and intensely hungry to get saved because her

oldest son, a former student at our High School, had lived true to holiness in the home. She told us for weeks she had been refraining from doing anything she thought would displease the Lord. After several times of earnest seeking, she found the Lord. Later, in a prayer meeting in her own home, she was beautifully sanctified.

"Great is the joy from having the privilege of helping souls to get ready to live for time; also for eternity. I am glad I ever heard and obeyed the call, 'Do the work of an evangelist.' "

An answer to a prevailing prayer of one of our pastors is related here:

"Someone has said that when God burdens our hearts He means to answer our prayers, if we are faithful in prayer. One time while our revival was in progress, I became so burdened after the Saturday night service that I could not retire, but wrestled in prayer until after one o'clock in the morning. The next morning God poured out His Spirit upon the Sunday School and the evangelistic service which followed, and two of the most influential men of the community were blessedly saved. Later when the one was being baptized, he wept and thanked God 'That the prayers of the righteous avail much.'

"He marveled and thanked God that He had saved him in spite of the fact that he had been brought up in a 'Hard Shell' doctrine. Sinners and wicked men stood on the river bank and wept."

"Oftentimes the dear people are misled by strange

doctrines that seem to flourish for a time in the long-neglected Home Mission Field. However, the power of the true Gospel in prayer and message brings great relief to these misguided souls.

"God says, 'Call unto me, and I will answer thee, and shew thee great and mighty things, which thou knowest not.' Jer. 33: 3.

"One time a preacher in a certain false cult in our community announced that on a certain day he would handle a rattlesnake, and show them that God was with him and that God meant for men to have power over serpents. The day arrived and the people milled in from every creek and hollow to see the great event. The little churchhouse was filled to overflowing with curious folk. My heart was greatly burdened. If this man should succeed, then many poor souls would be deceived and misled and believe this to be God's way. I went to the woodshed and prayed and asked God to open people's eyes and make an example of this false doctrine, for the sake of poor lost souls. The burden finally lifted and I went back to the house and watched the crowd come home from the meeting. All were excited. The snake handler had been bitten, and his arm was swollen to three times its normal size and was still swelling. They called in their crowd to pray for him declaring that God would heal him. The unsaved brother also called in a doctor who barely saved the man's life. Needless to say, that man has never handled any more snakes. Neither has anyone else been so foolish here. Truly our God hears and answers prayer. Truly, 'He will loose the bands of wickedness.' " Isa. 58: 8.

Here is an example of hand-picked fruit at a station in the South District.

"One evening after we had settled down to read, we were disturbed by the sound of a woman crying hard, almost screaming, and calling on the Lord. It came from the near neighbor's house, but we were at a loss to know what it was all about. Our first thought was that the husband of the youngest daughter, who at the time was home on a visit, must have been killed or hurt in the mines. We hesitated to go over, so prayed at our house. That was in divine order. After an hour or so the daughter came after us saying, the son's wife visiting in the home was dying. We went over and she wasn't dying, but was under awful conviction and crying for mercy. The family are Tongues people and had been praying and crying but couldn't get anywhere. They thought the girl sure-enough was dying. We immediately sensed both the presence of the Lord and also of the enemy. The girl was shaking—I suppose in Tongues' manner. It reminded me of what we read about in the Cane Ridge revival in Peter Cartwright's day. The marvel to me was the wonderful way in which we felt the Lord and His power over the enemy, and how easy it was to pray in faith for the enemy to be defeated as we pleaded the name of Jesus. We told her she would not die, but just to confess her sins and trust the Lord. In perhaps about ten minutes, the

girl prayed through and was saved. What a calm
after the storm! We felt the Lord ordered it thus as
an object lesson—'the god who answereth by fire,
let Him be God,' was the feeling we had."

One of our newest stations has had some rich victories. The pastor writes:

"Our station was opened about three years ago
with three workers living in a little two-room log
cabin, and holding services in a schoolhouse. God
has marvelously worked in our behalf since that
time. Land has been given for a church and parsonage. A well has been drilled and now we are waiting
for the buildings to be erected. We also have a lovely
four-room house, rent-free, in which to live while
we are waiting for the building to be done.

"The three revivals and the steady preaching of
the Word have brought light and help to the people
and God has definitely saved and sanctified precious
souls here. One promise He is fulfilling—given several months before our last revival—is, 'Thus saith
the Lord; Refrain thy voice from weeping and thine
eyes from tears: for thy work shall be rewarded,
saith the Lord; and they shall come again from the
land of the enemy.' Jer. 31: 16. Souls were saved and
sanctified in that second revival and we believe that
'the end is not yet.' Another good promise given to
encourage our faith is in Matthew 18: 18, 'Again I
say unto you, That if two of you shall agree on earth
as touching any thing that they shall ask, it shall be
done for them of my Father which is in heaven.' One

One of Kentucky Mountain Holiness Association Churches

Two of the Outstation Circuit Riders of
Kentucky Mountain Holiness Association

dear saint, who found the Lord in our meetings, has gone to heaven, leaving behind a rich and definite testimony to two works of grace.

"God has answered prayer time and again in taking charge of the order and in getting the attention of the congregation centered upon the Word. Interest in missions has been unusual for a new station. Offerings were given for this purpose even before a prayer band had been established.

"During one of our revivals the enemy sent in an opposer to holiness just as one of the converts was seeking to be sanctified. Things were at a standstill for two nights. We held a fast prayer meeting and God gave the victory. The opposer left the meeting and two converts were sanctified that night. We praise God for the definite answers to prayer which He has given; and we believe the future holds many more as we walk with Him."

Such choice souls are constantly being sought and found because they are ripe and ready to yield to the Lord. These encouragements do lift our faith and bring great glory to Jesus.

The following account shows a clear case of salvation resulting from the mid-week services:

"The Holy Ghost came upon our prayer services mightily. Conviction seized a lady. After the altar call was given, laying her sleeping child on the seat, she made her way to the altar. After praying quietly to herself, the workers assisting as best they could, she went home unsatisfied.

"The next morning as we were going to prayer meeting, one of her relatives, working in a field, called to us saying, 'Did you hear about Widow ——?' We said that we hadn't. Then he remarked, 'I reckon she must have gotten saved. I heard her coming down out of the hollow shouting.' Instead of having prayer meeting at the schoolhouse, we decided to go to this lady's house for prayer that morning. On our way there we met groups of people coming from her house, some with looks of disapproval. Gathered at her home were a number of neighbors. With a shining face she sat shouting the praises of God. We knew that a great change had taken place —that she had 'passed from death unto life.'

"We learned that early that morning she had gone out to feed her chickens, taking her little girl with her. The Lord spoke to her, telling her to go to a certain place, a short distance from the house, to pray. She obeyed and in a few minutes God spoke peace to her soul.

"The service that day was a glorious one. The Holy Ghost was there and took complete charge. Intermingled with our prayers and praises to God were her exhortations to the unsaved to get right with God. What a miracle of grace! He says, 'Call unto Me, and I will answer thee, and shew thee great and mighty things, which thou knowest not.' Jer. 33: 3.

"At the beginning of my station work, my co-worker and I lived in a dark, damp, little house, without any foundation and with a leaky roof. It was a precious place to us because the Holy Ghost met our hearts so richly there as we prayed for the spiritual needs of our people. However, we felt we could serve the people better if we had a more healthful home and one nearer the center of the community. We made this a matter of earnest prayer, also asking the Lord for a church building. A mountain man kindly gave a plot of ground on a lovely hillside in a good location. We praised God for this. Within two years He provided enough money to build a little parsonage. How thankful we were for such a comfortable home.

"In the midst of our rejoicing over this answer to prayer, the temptation came to feel that we had been selfish in desiring a nicer place to live when the funds could have been applied on a church. For years the Christians had been praying for a church, yet we were still worshiping in the schoolhouse. I went to prayer, telling the Lord we had wanted this house only for His glory, and that I knew He was abundantly able to supply the need for a church also. We continued prayer for the church. The people of the community intended to donate some lumber for it, but were unable to meet the financial needs.

"One day the Holy Ghost gave me these words, 'This people say, The time is now come, the time that the Lord's house should be built . . . Thus saith the Lord of hosts; . . . Go up to the mountain and bring wood and build the house; and I will take pleasure in it, and I will be glorified, saith the Lord.' Hag. 1: 2, 7, 8. For a week or more, the Holy Ghost burned

that promise into my soul. I reveled in it and was
mightily blessed. It was a mountain-top experience.
That was in the fall. The following spring Miss Mc-
Connell and a group spoke in a certain service up
North. At its close, the pastor said he felt led that
he and his congregation should donate the money
for a church building in our station. Again we rejoiced that God had answered our cries and those
of the faithful Christians. In less than six months,
the church was built and dedicated. Praise God!"

One of the National Holiness Missionary Society
Prayer Band representatives, Miss Miriam Gregory,
who spent five years with us, was visiting some of
our K. M. H. A. Prayer Bands. The pastors there had
been dealing with a lady in their parish about her
soul. The Prayer Band service began. A few of the
Christians had offered prayer. It was time for the
speaker to take charge. This hungry soul began to
pray. It was not long until she found Jesus precious
to her soul. She is so true to Jesus and a shining light
in her home and community. Many times in our
visitation and regular services we see lovely hand-
picked fruit like this.

––––––––––

*Another pastor writes of his experiences and ob-
servations in the Kentucky Mountain Holiness Association:*

"In February of 1944, I was sent of the Lord and
by the officials of the K. M. H. A. to an outpost station
on Devil's Creek in Wolfe County. There my wife
and I labored as pastors among many of my old ac-

quaintances and relatives. After about twenty-one months of labor, there came an urgent appeal from the headquarters to conduct a revival meeting in one of our new stations. After having prayed about it, wife and I felt that it was the leading of God that I should go. I found, after having arrived, that it was very much in need of the gospel. Some of the older residents thought it would be unwise for us to try to have night services. A few years previous to that time there was so much moonshine liquor made on that creek that it was dangerous for a person to be out after dark. Two of the neighbors were talking in regard to the meeting. They were in sympathy with the work being done, were hospitable and willing to feed and entertain the workers, but they said they did not intend to go to even one night meeting. They thought that the bad boys would tear up the meeting. However, we felt God leading us to go forward. The man was there the first night, and came every night after that and helped to keep order. The woman was there the second night and each night afterwards.

"The pastors had been going from an adjoining station, crossing a very steep hill on their way. They had done splendid foundation work during the short time they had been working there. The first service began on a Sunday afternoon. God's presence was felt in our midst. The next service was in the evening of the same day. Again God manifested His presence in a marvelous way. When the altar call was given, a young woman was the first to come for-

ward. Others followed until about eight souls were
bowing at the altar seeking God. A goodly number
of those testified to having found Jesus in His saving
grace. As time went on, our souls were blessed as we
ministered to the people in holy things. From time
to time, a goodly number of folk would come seeking
God. Needless to say, those who met conditions
found that for which their hearts had been hunger-
ing. They would rise from the altar with their faces
aglow and a testimony on their lips. As is com-
monly the case with truly regenerated persons,
where they have the light on holiness, most of the
converts were soon ready to seek the second blessing. Folk were surprised and delighted to see the
great change which had been wrought in such a
short length of time. I have seldom gone into a community where I have been more cordially received
as an evangelist.

"During the meeting around fifteen or twenty
testified to having been saved, and the most of those
also witnessed to having been sanctified. At the
close of that revival the community hardly seemed
like the same Creek. It was marvelous what a
change there was in the congregational singing, with
the new converts singing in the Spirit. Such music
furnished moving inspiration to the unsaved. We
sang that chorus, 'Since Jesus has come to our town,
The devil has been wearing a frown, Many hearts
have been changed, Many homes rearranged, Since
Jesus has come to our town.' These words did not
exactly suit since this was not a town and so some-

one revised the song so that it went something like this,

> 'Since Jesus has come to our creek,
> We're singing each day of the week.
> Many lives have been changed, many homes
>   rearranged,
> Since Jesus has come to our creek.'

It was wonderful to hear those people sing out God's praises after Jesus had so marvelously manifested Himself to them.

"The next year, in the summer of 1945, I was scheduled to conduct another revival. I was happily surprised to find that through faithful labors the ground had been prepared and the seed sown. The people were eager for God and the place was ready for a harvest time.

"It was decided that the best plan for carrying on the revival would be for the pastor, a student at K.M.B.I., to set up temporary living quarters in an old house near the schoolhouse, where we were to have the meeting. We would go out from there in the daytime and do personal work, and also conduct prayer meetings and have our regular services at night. For about two years the pastor had been faithfully praying and working, with the assistance of others from the Kentucky Mountain Bible Institute.

"The first service began on a Sunday morning, and God's smile of approval was upon it and us. The break came the next day, when a man of the community prayed through out in the corn field. He came to the prayer meeting and prayed and rejoiced and almost preached, he was so happy. His son, about sixteen years old, sought God in that same prayer meeting and was graciously saved.

"Conviction continued to spread. Others sought God and gave clear evidence of having found Him. One dear old lady attended. Her heart was desiring salvation. She came to the altar one night and was blessed and gave her testimony, though she did not state what the condition was which she had met and which had brought her relief. However, she later testified that she went home that night and threw away her pipe. She said she had not even wanted it since, though she had been smoking since she was a girl. A young lady who had waited for years for someone else to lead the way, made the start and was marvelously saved and sanctified. She immediately, with others, zealously began witnessing and working for the Lord. The joy of the Lord was our strength. Another thing which was especially gratifying was the fact that all the converts, except one, testified to being sanctified wholly. The series of meetings closed in triumph, and we went away with the assurance that God was still on the throne and answered prayer. This also was sure evidence that the days of revival were not over."

A Holy Ghost Revival is reported by one of our evangelists:

" 'And the God of Peace shall bruise Satan under

your feet shortly.' This was the promise quickened
to the writer in response to the prayer for some particular portion of Scripture upon which to stand in
a certain revival a few years ago. To her it was God's
definite Word for that particular situation. But as
she was inexperienced in revivals and not a particularly forceful character anyway, not much was
thought of the verse until a few days later when the
evangelist, a mature, powerful woman preacher received the same promise while praying out in the
little hillside church and shouted over it for an hour
straight. The many folk living in the valley knew
that someone had heard from heaven, but likely
knew nothing of what it was all about. But, without
question, in the realm of wicked spirits an alarm was
sounded; for the God of heaven was assuring His
intercessor on earth that one of their strong citadels
was about to fall. Strong citadel it was, for if ever
the enemy was intrenched and if ever sin was ugly,
blatant, and vicious, it was in that little community.
As the unlawful deeds and filthy conversation of an-
cient Sodom and Gomorrah caused the righteous
soul of Lot to be vexed from day to day, so the flaunt-
ing of hideous sins and the flow of vile language not
only caused the souls of a small group of sanctified
folk to be vexed, but to be much upon their faces before God in an agony of intercessory prayer. Strange
to say, at least strange to those not particularly ac-
customed to the work of soul-saving, not much was
accomplished outwardly in the above-mentioned revival except that God's people were graciously blest

and a few girls and children rather half-heartedly
sought the Lord. In fact, for three or four years other
revivals followed, some with a good bit of stir, but
none with any great depth of lasting good.

"The weary months rolled steadily on. The enemy
held on tenaciously. The little group of sanctified
believers prayed faithfully. Frequently only four or
five met together to weep and pray for souls. Surely
it looked as if no one cared. Few even bothered to
come to church on Sunday nights, and altogether too
often those who did come were of the wrong kind.
At times rocks were hurled against the sides of the
building, and occasionally they crashed through the
windows shattering the glass and the nerves of the
women on the inside. On one occasion when the
writer was present assisting in a second revival, one
of these missiles found its mark on the back of her
neck. Many times the believers were reminded that
one whose existence modernists deny, but of whom
John speaks as 'the dragon, that old serpent, which
is the devil, and Satan' was extremely busy, perhaps
because he felt his time would soon be short. At
times it seemed as if one of his cohorts was sitting on
every fence-post up and down the road.

"But the faithful God had not forgotten to be
gracious. He, whose eyes are over the righteous and
whose ears are open to their cries, had not missed a
tear or a prayer. And interestingly enough, the in-
tercessors had neither grown weary nor discouraged. With difficulties and delays, faith became pure
and strong, and expectancy ran high. Upon arising

from their knees, each encouraged the other with, 'It's coming! It is surely coming!' To their friends they wrote, 'God is going to give us a revival.' One might well wonder what outward evidence they had upon which to base their faith. There was none. For that matter, that which depends on circumstances and outward signs is not faith anyway.

"An evangelist was engaged, the same song-leader called back for the third time, and a date for the beginning of a revival was set. No time was set upon which to close the meeting, however; for the slogan of the Christians was 'Four or five weeks if necessary, or until things really break through.'

"The day arrived; the workers were on hand; services began. What was it that caused one's heart to beat high with joy almost instantly upon arriving on the ground? The unmistakable presence of the God of Peace! He had come! Come to bruise Satan! There was no doubting it from the start! As the Word speaks of the Spirit of God moving upon the face of the waters long ago, so anyone with any spiritual understanding at all knew the Spirit of God was moving upon the face of that community. The people poured into the church. The prayer meetings were times of powerful united praying in the Holy Ghost—times of definite praying through to fresh assurance of victory—times of being bold in claiming the defeat of the devil—bold in claiming souls for God.

"Each night as the people gathered in, it was to see the mighty power of the Holy Ghost settle down

on souls, often to see them grow pale, then rise and
find their way to an altar of prayer. Almost every
night souls sought and found God. And the seeking
was not usually long-drawn out, but exceedingly
intense and earnest. Frequently the groans and
prayers and even the screams of the penitent were
turned to shouts of victory before the altar call was
officially closed or the Christians had gathered
around for prayer. Husbands and wives prayed
through side by side. Fathers, mothers, sons, and
daughters alike wept their way to Jesus and arose
praising a mighty Christ for Blood-bought deliverance from sin. Nor did souls stop with simply the
deliverance from the guilt and power of sin, but prac-
tically every one who prayed through to the first
work, returned to lay hold on God for the deliverance from the nature of sin; for this was a holiness
revival.

"The little valley echoed again and again with the
shouts of the new-born babes in Christ, or the shouts
of some soul beholding for the first time the glories
of Canaan Land, or the shouts of some older saint
whose heart was fairly bursting with the joy of the
Lord. One factor ever present before the interces-
sors was that they be exceedingly careful not to
touch the glory. It was God! Everyone knew it was
God, and His alone was the glory! At times the presence of God was so rich that His people almost feared
to speak or pray lest they be hasty or thoughtless and
in anywise grieve or hinder the Spirit and the gracious work should cease.

"The revival which was to have lasted four or five weeks or until things broke through, came to a close in two weeks. The Christians were agreed that what was ready for gleaning at that time was in the garner, and that it was time to close. But properly speaking, the revival has not stopped. The out-pourings of the Spirit on some of the regular services since that time have surpassed even those which were manifested during the two-week revival period.

"The converts in this community have much about them that resembles the Apostolic Christians. As it was true of the Thessalonians to whom Paul wrote, 'For ye brethren, became followers of the churches of God which in Judea are in Christ Jesus; for ye also have suffered like things of your own countrymen, even as they have of the Jews,' so it is with these precious Christians, all of them suffering persecution at the hands of unsaved relatives and neighbors. But it may also be said of them as it was of those in apostolic times, 'The disciples were full of joy and the Holy Ghost.' They carry much soul burden for loved ones and neighbors, as well as for foreign missions, for which cause they also give liberally of their means. (Tithing was of course one of the by-products of such a revival).

"But as one of the Christians put it, 'Sin isn't blatant around here any more.' Although not everyone is saved, it is safe to say that the entire community has felt the effects of a mighty Holy Ghost revival. The God of Peace is still in the business of bruising Satan under the feet of His people."

V

"NONE OF THESE THINGS MOVE ME"

"Therefore, my beloved brethren, be ye stedfast, unmovable, always abounding in the work of the Lord, forasmuch as ye know that your labour is not in vain in the Lord." I Cor. 15:58.

One of our own girls whom the Lord has mightily used among her own people, was holding a revival in one of our pastorates. She felt led to preach on holiness for several nights. All the people in the community that were ready for the blessing got over into Canaan. This, as always, stirred the enemy. A man came riding up the ridge one day and said to her, "Young woman, you keep on preaching like that, and the bad boys of the community will make a run of moonshine out under the cliff and come here and break up your 'meetin'." Sure-enough the boys came riding over the mountains, shooting their guns in the air and yelling. They came into the service filling up all the back of the room. The evangelist was sitting on the front seat while the song leader was conducting the first part of the service. The devil came to her and said, "Now this is the night that you are going to get cut up with a knife." She was not much afraid of guns, but she always had a horror of the big knives that some of the boys carry. She fought the enemy for awhile and finally said, "Mr. Devil, if that is God's plan, I am ready." The enemy left her. She had great liberty in preaching. God took charge of her and also controlled the young men.

Sometimes after we start a revival, an opposition crowd will begin a meeting in the neighborhood. We go right on preaching, believing God, and honoring the Holy Ghost.

A certain source that the Lord had raised up to send us an offering each year failed. The one in charge said this group could not do it any more on account of the depression. I knew that the money given to us came from the tithes and offerings of the people, and that it was only because the leader did not want to help us. After I had heard from one of our very dear friends who loves our work and has stood by us through the years, that this offering would not be taken, I went into the back classroom at the Mt. Carmel High School and prayed. It took me only a few minutes to get victory over this fearful disappointment. God assured me that He would supply the need. That year God sent us more money than in any previous year. "Have faith in God." Mark 11: 22.

With our food bills more than $10,000 each year in our two boarding schools and with many other running expenses, it keeps us with our hearts and minds stayed on Jesus. God's faithfulness is grand. It grows on us year after year. It is good to have the wheels of faith unclogged, so that you can pray your way out of each trial or dilemma. An all-conquering faith laughs at impossibilities and cries, it shall be done.

A dear man who had a very bad record lived in one of the communities where we had services. Everyone warned us that he would do us harm and drive us out of the place. There were five men killed near where he lived. He made and sold liquor all the time. We went trusting fully in the Lord to help us to reach him. God moved on his heart. He gave us a house to live in and before the summer was over one of his sisters came to visit him and said, "You are not going to hurt the missionaries or drive them out." He said, "No, I'm not. I believe in their kind of religion and I'm going to see to it that no one else drives them out." He is our friend today. Beloved, none of these things move us, because God is on our side.

The following are some of the outstation experiences of one of our pioneer workers:

"During my first summer in station work, I was to take my turn first in the preaching. This was on Sunday night. The people told us that it was impossible to hold night meetings. In fact, two of the men had drawn their knives in the morning, arguing over the place where we should have the service.

"As I stood to give the message, in my mind's eye I could see missiles of every nature flying through the little schoolhouse windows, but the Lord helped me to sweep on past any fears, and gave such gracious liberty that the audience of sixty or seventy people who had crowded into the little schoolhouse, were as respectful and quiet as anyone could wish,

A Graduating Class of Kentucky Mountain Bible Institute

Inside View of Myers Memorial Chapel of Kentucky Mountain
Bible Institute

much to the amazement of the people themselves. This continued throughout the summer. In our revival meeting, fifteen people sought the Lord in saving grace and thirteen of them went on to seek holiness. One precious young woman arose to testify shortly after the Lord had saved her. She said, 'You folk all know me, and that I have been baptized three times trying to find peace for my soul, but tonight at this altar God has given me the peace I have sought so long. Now, I want to be baptized again for I feel that this is the first time I have really been ready for it.'

"We were holding a revival meeting in the schoolhouse at one of our outstations. A mountain preacher from some distance away had said that he was going to preach there on the last Sunday of our meeting. The schoolhouse was packed, so that my co-worker and I had to sit on top of one of the desks during his preaching. The man said that they called him the 'fighting preacher' and that he was proud of it. He proceded to tear to pieces the evangelist's message of the morning, and to incriminate the missionaries. He told the people that they could starve us all out of the country by locking their chicken houses and hiding their pocket books, and that they were not to attend our meeting. We had to leave before the service was over to walk three miles over the mountain to another service in the afternoon.

"When we returned late that afternoon, the people all along the trail came out to invite us to their homes for supper. One man said that he could not understand how we ever took what the fellow said. Our evangelist answered that he had the experience of perfect love in his heart and that he had no hard feelings against the man whatever. This was something new for a people inclined to get revenge. That night the house was crowded to capacity, with many who could not get in. They wanted to know more about the salvation that could keep folk sweet under such railing accusations, unjust as they were. We could understand then why the people kept turning to look at us as my co-worker and I sat on the desk in the morning service. God so graciously gave us grace and blessing and the favor of the people, that we would have willingly gone through the experiences again if He could get glory thereby. Suffice it to say, the dear mountain preacher evidently saw that God was with us, and he has been kind to us ever since.

"It was my privilege to be one of the pioneer workers at another of our outstations. We experienced mighty outpourings of the Spirit during those summer months there. God honored the preaching of His Word on saving grace and sanctifying power, and some of the folk became hungry for the experience of heart holiness. One day when we were getting ready to go out calling, two precious mothers in the community came down the road in great agony of soul. As soon as they entered the house one of them cried out that she felt she must be sanctified that very day. We knelt to pray, and in less than ten minutes, the faithful Holy Ghost met her heart. She wept and rejoiced. With her finger tips striking our low ceiling with every shout of joy, she gave glory to Jesus for the cleansing of her carnal heart.

"During the revival another mother was among the seekers. The Lord saved her one night, and befor breakfast the next morning, two mountain preachers went to her home and said to her that they were glad that she had 'got religion' the night before, but that she was to leave 'that thar holiness' alone! Her answer to them was that she had been saved one time before, but that she had backslidden because she had failed to get rid of the carnal nature. Now she had gotten saved the night before so that she she could go on and get sanctified. She was at the morning prayer meeting seeking for the experience. Of course, God met her hungry soul as she confessed out her need of a clean heart. This experience gave her grace to stand under the fearful taunts of an ungodly husband, and made her a witness for God and holiness in her own home and in the community. Beloved, holiness works."

Here is how another pastor proved the Word of God and won many victories:

"When God led me to stay in the Mountains He gave me the promise, Isaiah 41: 10, 'Fear thou not; for I am with thee: be not dismayed; for I am thy God: I will strengthen thee; yea, I will help thee; yea, I will uphold thee with the right hand of my righteousness.' How often has this promise been renewed to me through the years. There have been

many times when I have been a bit fearful, but when
God would remind me of this promise my courage
was renewed. What a tower of strength this promise
has been to me. Just to know that God is with us in
times of danger means everything.

"One night after service two young women came
to us and asked us to walk home with them, saying
that they were afraid, since a man was there that had
threatened to kill them. We felt led to go with them,
feeling confident that God would take care of us. On
our way home with them we passed the man that
they feared, and he glared at us fiercely, but made
no move to touch us. We took the young women up
the dark branch and arrived safely at their home.
When we turned from their door to go to our home,
the Lord spoke to us and said, 'The wise men departed into their own country another way.' We did
not know why, but felt that God wanted us to go
home another way. We crossed the branch and
crawled under a barbed wire fence and wended our
way around the hillside, going through briar patches
and crawling through many barbed wire fences. We
finally arrived home safely. The next day we learned
that the enraged man had hired boys to stone us
when we came back down the branch. But God gave
us wisdom and we escaped the stones.

" 'Peter therefore was kept in prison: but prayer
was made without ceasing of the church unto God
for him.' Acts 12: 5.

"It helps much to have God's people everywhere
praying for us. God answers your prayers if you are

truly abiding in Him and His words abiding in you. As you abide in Him, He entrusts you with burdens and when you pray faithfully, He answers.

"One night I was sitting up with a dying woman. About nine o'clock she died. The folk asked me to lay her out. I had never laid anyone out in my life and felt I just could not do it. Yet, I felt I did not dare to refuse because they would not understand. A missionary is supposed to know how to do everything. I was all in a tremble. I lifted my heart to God in silent prayer, and suddenly calmness stole over me. I knew He had given me the grace and strength. I went ahead just as though I had been at the undertaking business all my life. God wonderfully helped me. A few days later I received a letter from a friend saying, 'On such a night (giving date) I felt burdened to pray for you. Were you in great need?' I found that it was the very night that I had needed special help and grace to lay out the dead."

Prevailing prayer made these pastors unmoveable.
"Our church at Consolation outstation was built during war times, yet carpenters from other states were willing to leave good jobs and give labor here. Material for the building came just as it was needed. Much to our surprise, someone sent us a washing machine to help launder the clothes of the builders.

"In the first revival held in the new church, souls were getting light on sanctification. The attendance was large and the people attentive. A crowd of boys was prompted by the enemy to break up the meeting. A night or so these boys marched around the church trying to draw a bead on the lights. Through a friend this was made known to us. In the Saturday morning prayer meeting the Lord assured us all that we would not be molested any longer.

"That evening I was informed that the two leaders of the rough gang had been stricken with sickness at ten o'clock that morning. God heard when His children prayed, and gave victory over opposition. The meeting closed after several folk had found the Lord.

"In the beginning days of this station a man and his wife were sanctified. This couple were living good justified lives, but lacked power to testify and break away from opinions of the world. When the Holy Ghost came, their hearts were cleansed of the man-fearing spirit and filled with perfect love and boldness to stand persecution. Also this family very readily gave up all dealings with tobacco crops. Since then their mountain farm always has a big crop of strawberries, potatoes, or corn. God is prospering them. They now testify that the tithe to the Lord is more than the income tobacco used to bring. Their free and fearless stand for righteous living brought a revival. Others sought to be saved, reclaimed, or sanctified. Even those who had strong prejudices against the experience of holiness of heart were freed from their unbelief and filled with the Holy Ghost.

"The preaching of purity of mind, soul, and body still brings revivals. Periodically, seasons of conviction sweep over this valley; a revival comes, and souls get victory from all sin. 'Thine, O Lord, is . . . the glory, and the victory.' I Chron. 29: 11.

"Joyous praise goes up from our hearts for the sanctified families and individuals, scattered upon the mountains, who are letting His Truth triumph through them.

"In these past years of station work the Lord has indeed given abundant strength. His promises have been satisfying, and victory has been perpetual. During the first summer here at Consolation, our menu for a few days was reduced to potatoes and beans. I thanked God over and over for my appetite for beans, but felt as if He could give us a change. The Lord gently reminded me that there was always plenty in His cupboard and I should have asked for my needs before we got so low. My helper and I decided we would not let them know at headquarters, but we would really see if we could live by faith. We fasted and prayed. The next day some friends from Ohio were passing through on their way south; feeling impressed to see us, they came our way for a short visit. Before they left we were given a large box in which we found a ham, bacon, fresh fruit, vegetables, and cake. The Lord supplied all our needs and even the extras. That summer thoughtful friends sent a sewing machine and a heater for the parsonage, and an organ for the church."

The dear people in some sections have been misled by strange doctrines. We pray for them truly to come to Jesus and be made happy in Him and enjoy salvation so that they will live normal, happy, Christian lives. We never mention or preach against these strange ideas into which someone has led them. We do our best to live before the people and love them good and preach the precious Word of Truth. God has used this method to help these misguided souls. It is the Truth that kills out the false every time.

One of our high school girls attended a "Snake Handling" meeting in the mountains near her home. She said they worked themselves into a frenzy at the beginning of the service. The leader then said, "Is anyone ready to trust the Lord and handle these snakes?" To prove from the Bible they take this verse in Mark 16: 18, "They shall take up serpents; and if they drink any deadly thing it shall not hurt them." There was a box of snakes on the platform in the little schoolhouse. A timid little woman came to the box, got out a snake, and wrapped it around her neck. Others came, men and women, until there were a number of the people carrying the snakes around. They would twine them around their necks, fondle them, and hug them to their bosoms. She said it was a very gruesome sight. How they need the true gospel!

The wife of one of our dear pastors relates the glories of pioneer work in one of the first permanent stations. They pastored this place for five years. She and her husband were teaching in our Kentucky Mountain Bible Institute when the Flash Flood of July, 1939 swept it all away. The marvelous grace of God has sustained her ever since the "home going" of her three darling children and her sainted husband who lost their lives in the flood. She has been teaching in our Bible School ever since her life was spared, after having been tossed in the fearful torrent of a twenty-foot wall of water down Frozen Creek and *up* the Kentucky River for a few miles.

"Soon after our marriage at Mt. Carmel we were appointed to the Index station. My heart is blessed and filled with praise to the Lord for the five gracious years which He gave us there. My dear husband finished building the parsonage which was already begun, and we were privileged to be the first to live in it. There the Lord gave us two precious little boys and blessed our home life with His love and presence. The confidence of knowing we were in His will and called to a definite holiness ministry, solved many problems for us and enabled us to trust God for answers to prayer.

"Although the work was comparatively new in the community, there was already a group of saved and sanctified people who loved the Lord and were under the burden for souls. As we mingled our prayers and praises, God poured out His Spirit upon us. Especially, I recall how He met with us in the cottage prayer meetings which were held in various homes. Surely 'heaven came down our souls to greet.' Faithful attendance at the prayer meetings kept the joy of the Lord rich in the hearts of the Christians, and brought fresh blessing on the other services. Through the months and years, God honored the faithful preaching of His Word in the message of full salvation, and the Holy Ghost dealt with souls. Some of them sought the Lord in the regular services while many were saved and sanctified wholly in the revivals.

"In one revival conviction settled powerfully on the people. One night the service was dismissed without anyone yielding, but with deep conviction on hearts. A few Christians remained at the church to pray. One young woman went home, but was under such a burden for a neighbor girl that she could not sleep. Her father walked with her about a half mile to the other girl's home. They brought her back to the church where she prayed through to gracious victory. Numbers of other young people were saved in that same revival. Eleven boys and girls out of one Sunday School class were saved and some of them sanctified. One night it rained so hard that scarcely anyone came to the service, but one young married woman came under much conviction. She confessed her sins and was wonderfully saved that night. In a few days the Lord sanctified her and gave her a burden for her husband. She prayed until he too found the Lord.

"Among others, two of the outstanding converts of those years were two heads of families—men who ever since then have walked steadily with God and honored the Holy Ghost. Today their lives are counting mightily for God's glory. One of them now lives in another state, but is a great blessing in his community. The other, with his precious sanctified wife, is one of the pillars of the Index church.

"As the saints grew in grace they became missionary-minded and we felt led to organize a missionary prayer band. We rejoiced to see them walk in the light as God gave them vision and burden for the lost. At one of the first meetings a dear sanctified woman said she felt impressed that they should give a definite offering to missions. They agreed to pledge twenty-five dollars for the support of a Chinese student. Another lady spoke at once and said, 'I have just nine cents. It's not tithe but you are welcome to it.' With that nine cents our first missionary project was launched. At the same meeting a new convert testified that she had received light on tithing and wanted to give a dollar. It was precious to see how quickly the Lord enabled them to play that pledge. Sometime later at another prayer meeting, we announced that the twenty-five dollars was all in with the exception of about forty cents. The same dear woman who gave the first nine cents said, 'Praise the Lord. I have enough to finish it!' How much the Lord blessed her!

"This is only an example of the way the fulness of the blessing was manifested in their hearts. They not only prayed and gave sacrificially to foreign missions, but many times they surprised us with loving gifts of food, pasture for our cow, and then also hauled our coal and helped in many ways. The Lord so wonderfully took care of us, supplying our food, clothing, fuel, and incidental expenses. In times of sickness, the Lord laid it on hearts far and near to send us money to pay our doctor and hospital bills.

Many times our hearts were melted in praise and
gratitude for all His goodness to us. To be sure, there
were times when our faith was tested, but those were
times of unusual blessing.

"The Lord took care of us and blessed our hearts
continually. We found it a joy to live by faith and
counted it a privilege to serve the Lord in the beauty
of holiness. The memory of those happy years is
precious to me now since my loved ones went to
heaven in the Flash Flood of July, 1939. My loving
companion is already enjoying the reward of his
faithful labors. As we shared the burdens and the
blessings then, we will rejoice together through all
eternity over the victories and give honor and glory
to Jesus for salvation through His precious Blood.

"I love the Lord with all my heart and praise Him
that He ever called me to the hills of Kentucky for
life. I love my call and have found perfect joy and
peace in the center of His will. He has given grace
and glory every step of the way and the comfort of
the precious Holy Ghost is rich in my heart today."

One of our mountain girls writes:
"These years of experience in the Kentucky Mountain Holiness Association have flamed the fire of perfect love in my soul, stiffened my spiritual backbone,
and largely increased my faith for the salvation of
those around me.

"During the summer months of my Sophomore
year in Mt. Carmel High School, I took my first pastorate. The blessing of full salvation was continually

bubbling over in my soul. One Sunday night while my co-worker was leading the singing a young man who was sitting two seats behind me suddenly shot into the aisle directly between us. Being a mountain girl, I refused even to look back or get much excited. I knew he was through and would do no more harm. He immediately rushed out of the house with the men after him. The rest of the congregation flocked around us for protection, crying and trembling like leaves. My co-worker knelt to pray and God helped me to comfort the hearts of the people. I encouraged them to take their seats and relax, that they were perfectly safe. I marched to the platform, took my text, and delivered the message under the blessing of God. 'He will give grace and glory.'

"After I had graduated from the Kentucky Mountain Bible Institute, the doctor discovered a small spot on one of my lungs. He put me to bed for three months. I was perfectly contented in His will. At the end of the three months there was no trace of the disease, nor has there been since. To God be all the glory.

"Last September in a car wreck one of my arms was broken and the other wrist was sprained, plus many licks and cuts on my body. Folk thought I would never walk again. Now, I feel no effects from all of this for which I praise the Lord. God has fulfilled the verse, 'Therefore, my beloved brethren, be ye stedfast, unmoveable, always abounding in the work of the Lord, forasmuch as ye know that your work is not in vain in the Lord.' " I Cor. 15:58.

A teacher tells of God's mighty comforting grace and wisdom in the Flash Flood of July, 1939.

"In the spring of 1939, I was praying for the Lord to give me His leadings for the summer months after school would be out. He showed me that He wanted me to remain at the Bible School, as I thought, to carry on the Sunday School and visit in the homes of the community of Vancleve. He gave me the promise in Isa. 41:13, 'For I the Lord thy God will hold thy right hand, saying unto thee, Fear not; I will help thee.' I didn't understand the real reason for the promise, but it was a great blessing to me and helped me to know that I was in the will of the Lord in staying at the school.

"On July 4, those of us who had stayed at the school, worked until noon, the men repairing the front porch of the main building, and the girls and I doing the house cleaning and cooking for the family. The afternoon was our holiday. At supper time the Myers' family and all of us had a picnic supper under the trees on the campus. Two nieces and a nephew of Mr. Myers came on the afternoon bus and enjoyed the picnic and social time with us. Just before dark great streaks of lightning rent the sky to the north of us, and we thought there would be a storm somewhere, but did not think it would be near us.

"About three o'clock in the night, I was awakened when rain came pouring down. I got up and closed all the windows in the house, and not knowing what else I could do, went back to bed. An hour or so later, I was suddenly aroused by a loud crash and the

sound of rushing water. Looking out my window,
I saw that our large three-story building was sur-
rounded by high water. The crash was evidently
that of a nearby house hitting our building and causing it to break loose from its foundation, though we
did not realize that at the time. It was getting light
outside, but was still dark in the house. I ran to the
door to call the girls, but found it was jammed so
that it would not open. The Lord was holding my
right hand, and so with a second jerk it came open.
By that time the girls were out in the hall praying
and crying to the Lord for help.

"Our gas lights were out and the whole south side
of the house was slanting down. Water covered the
first floor of the building and was nearly up to the
second floor where we were. In the midst of roaring
of the water below and the praying of the girls, I
cried out to the Lord and said, 'Lord, show us what
to do!' Immediately He answered and said, 'Go to
the attic!'

"I ran to get my flashlight and we went upstairs.
When we reached the top of the stairs, I flashed my
light back and saw that already the trunks on the
second floor, from which we had just come, were
floating around. The girls looked out the small attic
window and saw that we had floated about a mile
down the creek toward the river.

"As the water reached the attic floor the girls began climbing out the window, so that the roof would
not pen us in. Since Elsie could swim, she was the
first to go. Elsie had been saved and later sanctified

wholly while attending Mt. Carmel High School.
Her mother had been saved as a result of the change
in her life at home. She had had one year at Bible
School. Just before she climbed out she lifted up her
shining face to heaven and prayed, 'Lord, I've been
trusting Thee to take care of me and I trust Thee
now!' That was the last time we saw her alive, but
Jesus did take care of her, for He took her to be with
Himself. God bless her memory.

"Then timid Christine jumped into the surging
water. She had been with us only three weeks, but
during that time she had been saved and a few days
later the Lord had cleansed her heart from all carnality. As a result of the testimony which she wrote
home, her younger brother was saved and is now
preaching the gospel. Christine did not say anything
as she left us, but the Lord was with her and took
her straight home to glory.

"Just after Lorene had climbed out and I had put
my hand on the window sill ready to do the same,
the window closed. For an instant I thought I was
trapped inside the building, but the Lord was there
and helped me to get it open again. I put my head
out, but before I could climb out, the entire building
fell apart and I found myself floating in the water
clinging to the window sill. The side wall of the
building soon made a good raft, so I crawled on to it
and called Lorene, the only one I could see, to come
with me. We discovered that our building had been
washed about a mile and a half down the creek and
had then hit the bank and gone to pieces about a half

mile from the river. Lorene and I were going fast toward the river. We hit a snag which broke our raft in two pieces, with her on one part and me on the other part. I tried to catch hold of branches of trees to pull myself to shore, but could not. Soon I discovered a place where there were no trees. The water was far above the willows that usually line the banks.

"By this time I could see the river ahead and I realized there was no earthly help for me. The great rushing torrent of water was dashing against the opposite bank of the river and throwing it into the air about one hundred feet high. My only hope was in the Lord as I plunged into the midst of the whirling, dashing water. The next thing I knew I was under the water facing eternity. My heart rested in Jesus as I said, 'Lord, I've done the best I could. I trust Thee to take care of me.' I felt quiet and full of faith in Him. My next thought was that I must do something. I could feel a board bouncing on the top of my head, so I began to push it away. The next instant I came to the top of the water and grabbed hold of a piece of the building. I had been unconsciously holding my breath under the water, so that it took several minutes to get it back. Then I crawled on to my new raft and thanked the Lord for sparing my life. My heart was rejoicing, though I was not yet on the land, and though my raft was covered with trash and bugs of various kinds. It was not long before I realized that other pieces of buildings were in the river too and would soon knock me under again if I did not do something. I grabbed a long stick and used it to push these pieces from my raft, first on one side and then on the other side of me. When I could I reached for branches hanging over the river bank to try to pull myself ashore, but I wasn't a very good river man.

"In this manner I traveled down the Kentucky River for about eight miles. Shortly after getting on to this raft, I saw Lorene on a piece of driftwood and later on another one. The Lord had spared her life. We called back and forth to each other as we floated downstream. Then I missed her and didn't know whether she had been able to get ashore, or whether she had after all been pushed under, not to come up again. I found out later that she had pulled herself ashore at the foot of Mt. Carmel campus, which was about four miles from where our Bible School stood, and thus was able to give them word of what had happened.

"Sometime after that I passed two men standing on the bank. They called to a man across the river, who had a boat, to rescue me. They said they would help, but they could not reach me since I was not on their side of the river. I was unable to get to shore by myself. By this time the river was full of driftwood and debris of all kinds. It took a good boatman to stem the now rough and high river. Mr. Bob Griffith risked his life, his boat almost overturning, before he reached me. But the Lord was directing affairs and did not let that happen. Mr. Griffith brought me safely to shore at his sister's landing place. Mrs. Dora Lockard and her family were very kind in helping me get cleaned up and in giving me clean clothes. I could not get to Mt. Carmel that day because of the high water. My mind was still in a daze over all that had happened, but the Lord brought comfort to my heart in the words of the song, 'He is mine, mine, Blessed be His Name!' I was very conscious that it was the Lord that had brought me through. Though I don't understand why some were taken and some were spared, yet I do know that He knoweth best. My life is His, wholly and forever. The Holy Ghost is abiding in His fulness, and in a very real sense I say, 'My life is not my own; it was bought with a price.' "

Beloved, none of these things move us.

VI

PRAISE, JOY AND LOVE
STRENGTHEN FAITH

We cannot be happy ourselves without promoting the happiness of all others. "I will praise Thee with my whole heart . . . and praise Thy name for Thy lovingkindness and for Thy truth; for Thou has magnified Thy word above all Thy name." Psalm 138: 1, 2.

"He that dwelleth in the secret place of the most High shall abide under the shadow of the Almighty." Psalm 91: 1. Where love exists, secret communion will be sought under the greatest difficulties. Furthermore, love out of a pure heart gives us a compassionate love for humanity. This love manifested in giving our lives, as it were, a "living sacrifice" in His service for souls, proves our faith in Jesus. "He who loves God most, loves humanity most."

One great characteristic of our workers and Christians in the Kentucky Mountain Holiness Association is Praise. Rich seasons of rejoicing are heard in the testimony meetings and in the revival services. Often in their private devotions sweeps of joy and praise flood their souls so that they are enabled to go forth to meet the battles, and oftentimes hardships of the day. "The joy of the Lord is our strength."

Our June and Christmas conferences are times of praise and fellowship. All the pastors, evangelists, teachers, and helpers meet for two days at Mt. Carmel, our headquarters. We are refreshed and helped by the messages of some seasoned man or woman who comes to give us deep and powerful truths from the Word. Reports of the past six months are heard. Appointments are made. The profits gained spiritually from the conference studies are discussed. While all of our workers are well trained, yet for the benefit of refreshing our minds and hearts, we plan to have each one study a prescribed course of study every six months. We have two Bible themes, one book on missions, one holiness book, either doctrinal or biographical of a holiness leader like Wesley, Commissioner Brengle, H. C. Morrison, and others.

The products of our schools (we are now graduating from twenty-five to thirty each year) give us much reason to praise God and thus our faith takes hold more each year for greater results.

Through twenty-two years in this holiness center, great volumes of praise have been voiced through our annual camp meeting, missionary conventions, conferences, and commencements because it is through these gatherings that the pulse of the increase of the work is so manifest. Surely goodness and mercy have followed us through these years.

To encourage and bless our hearts *the Lord sends us many visitors all through the year*. They come from all parts of this country and from many foreign lands with their messages of power and blessing. The richness of God's Word interpreted to our hearts

back in these hills feeds our souls constantly. Among
these visitors have been: Rev. Joseph H. Smith, Dr.
H. C. Morrison, Dr. Iva D. Vennard, Dr. C. W. But-
ler, Dr. and Mrs. G. Arnold Hodgin, Rev. H. M.
Couchenour, Rev. C. W. Ruth, Rev. C. W. Troxel,
Dr. T. M. Anderson, Dr. G. W. Ridout, Dr. E. R.
Overly, Dr. Peter Wiseman, Dr. Warren C. McIntire,
Rev. and Mrs. Woodford Taylor, Dr. H. E. Jessop,
Dr. Z. T. Johnson, Dr. Paul Rees, Dr. Andrew John-
son, Rev. D. Willia Caffrey, and many others of our
National Holiness movement.

God is enabling us to keep faithfully laboring on
in spite of war, strikes, rationing, and global turmoil.
The admonition, "Rejoice evermore," and continual
praise through giving of thanks for everything have
been the bulwark of our faith.

Another great joy is to see our converts join the
Missionary Prayer Bands and give to missions. We
never take offerings for ourselves, but we do for foreign missions.

"Yesterday our Sunday School *offering for missions was $7.29,*" *writes one of our pastors.* "Our
people voted unanimously to give $100 for missions
this year. We just get blessed to pieces. The things
that once seemed impossible are becoming daily oc-
currences now. This year our Sunday School gave
$30.00 for Esther Faulkner's support (one of our
mountain girls who is now in India, $10.00 for Mar-
garet Thompson, and $10.00 for China. Oh, how we
do praise God for what He has done here.

"We are happy too about the Bibles. We have sold

a dozen already and it looks as if I am going to have to order more. A number of sinners, who have seen these of the Christians, are wanting them too, and some have already bought them.

"The Christians are all subscribing for the Pentecostal Herald and we are arranging a little library in the church, placing in it Brengle's books on holiness, some of Dr. H. C. Morrison's books, Bud Robinson's, etc. We want good books that they can understand and get blessed over. Our Christians are doing remarkably well leading our prayer meetings."

Another pastor writes: "In the spring of 1944, we felt the urge to 'lengthen our cords' and reach out farther with the precious messages of full salvation. We were already covering a large parish, contacting many families in our visitation program, but the Lord definitely led us to conduct services in a little schoolhouse about three and one-half miles across the hills. We know that when God calls, He enables. Occassionally we rode a neighbor's horse, but we usually walked, leaving home about 8:30 A. M. and returning in time for the afternoon service at our home station. God gave us strength to make these trips through snow, ice, rain, sleet, mud, and heat, missing only two Sundays the entire year.

"As we have obeyed His commands and lifted up a standard of holy living through the Word even though it meant much hardship, God has faithfully kept His part of the covenant. He has done the exceeding abundantly in supplying our spiritual and temporal needs, and best of all He has given us precious souls."

A new station is opened; the pastor reports as follows:

"The Lord has been working here. Hearts are very hungry. At our second Sunday evening service, two raised their hands for prayer. One man came to the altar. Last Sunday night eight asked for prayer. Several of these are heads of homes. One of these was the man who asked us to start a work here. Another man has lived a very wicked life, but is really hungry. We were in their home Sunday and found both of them wanting to get an experience. One of the women who raised her hand was the mother of this man. She has thirteen children and all are out in sin. The men of the community are standing back of the problems of order in the services, so we are not bothered with that, for which fact we are very thankful. We will be glad when we get some Christians to help pray and carry on the work. People are anxious for a permanent station here. Some of the men made some extra seats today; now we have enough for the crowds.

"In one or two days more we can visit all the homes in the community and then we will be ready to begin again. The houses are quite scattered. They have had no preaching along this creek for the last twenty years except two times during the summer when they have had memorial meetings in the graveyard. Children have never been in a Sunday

School before. The place has been neglected forever. We need your prayers."

Often folk need to *catch up in their praising in
order for the Lord to release His power* upon them.
In the second semester revival in the Mt. Carmel
High School we felt that was what the Lord would
have us to do. In one of our faculty prayer meetings,
I told the teachers that God had spoken to me about
praising Him even before the revival started. This
was before the evangelist arrived. The evangelist
was one of our young men who, with his wife, is holding one of our outstation pastorates, and is a graduate of our Kentucky Mountain Bible Institute. He
is an excellent, Spirit-filled preacher. He preached
the Word, not his own theories. Thus the Holy Ghost
used him to do his full share in the revival.

We had been burdened for some of the students
who were still unsaved and had prayed much for
them. Now was the time all through the revival to
praise God for the host of saved and sanctified students, for the good firm establishment of so many of
them, and for those who were answering the call
that God had put upon them. Our praises so richly
released Holy Ghost power and joy upon the faculty
and the students, that the Lord had full chance to
bless all who were on blessing ground. This too, gave
the evangelist much liberty and freedom in delivering the truth. God answers prayer through praise
as well as through burdens. Paul and Silas brought
God on the scene through their prayers, songs, and
shouts of praise. As a result, in the revival, many

souls prayed through. Some came to the altar day
after day until their hearts were completely satisfied.

It was indeed a glorious meeting. Some of the
young people would say, "I feel so blessed all the
time." They wondered why they had so little burden. In the boys' and girls' prayer meetings each
evening, we heard shouts and praises. They would
break out with songs again and again. God was
mightily upon the campus all through the entire
meeting. This verse was quickened to our hearts,
"For it is not ye . . . but the Holy Ghost." Mark
13: 11.

Many times we need to rejoice and praise the
Lord. The joy that flows over on others surely does
put them under conviction and make them hungry
for salvation. Joy and praise are a mighty asset to
one's faith.

Instances of joy and gladness and praise as given
in Acts: (1) Of the disciples in the temple, because
they had received the Holy Ghost, 2: 46, 47. (2) Of
the impotent man healed by Peter, 3: 8. (3) Of Paul,
when he went up to Jerusalem, 20: 22, 24. (4) Of
Paul and Silas in the jail at Philippi, 16: 25. (5) Of
Rhoda, when she heard Peter at the gate, 12: 14.
(6) Of the disciples at Jerusalem, when Peter told
them about the conversion of Cornelius and other
Gentiles, 11: 18. (7) Of Barnabas, when he saw the
success of the gospel at Antioch, 11: 22, 23. The infilling of the Holy Ghost brings great joy. "Now the
God of hope fill you with all joy and peace in believing, that ye may abound in hope, through the power

of the Holy Ghost." Rom. 15: 13. "In thy presence is fulness of joy." Psalm 16: 11.

The vast increase of joy that comes to the sanctified heart *makes believing prayer easier,* and helps to lead us into rich communion with the Lord. Enjoy the spirit of prayer, then there is no oppressive spirit upon you which is often the heaviness of temptation.

We find in our revivals here in the hills that when our souls are drawn out in prayer—not groaning, but rejoicing, these seasons are mostly followed with exceptional manifestations of saving power. Beloved, "The joy of the Lord is our strength" and our faith increases as our religious joy deepens. Mahan says, "Truth apprehended under the illumination of the Holy Ghost becomes as fire in our bones."

One of our evangelists, Rev. Martha L. Archer, who has been with us for twenty years, gives God much praise for the call and ministry here in the Kentucky Hills:

"In 1925, by the way of Asbury College, the Spirit led me to the mountains. In the first Mt. Carmel School revival ,through a gracious and heavenly visitation, the question came, 'Will you stay in the mountains the rest of your days?' My heart responded with a glad 'Amen' to the whole will of God for my life. Although that call was severely tested, yet thank God, His love in my heart triumphed.

"Now, after twenty years in the hills, I can testify to being supremely happy, endeavoring with the body of God's sanctified co-workers to spread Scriptural holiness in the Kentucky Mountains.

"In the early years of our work, the Spirit impressed my heart with the fact that evangelism was to be the cap sheaf of my ministry. Thus, after teaching in our schools, the summer months were given to revivals throughout the Association.

"Glancing back over the battlefield, we are constrained to shout, 'Elijah's God still lives today, and answers still by fire.' Many a mountain has been brought low by the assuring voice of our mighty Captain. 'As I was with Moses, so I will be with thee.' Josh. 1: 5. We believed it! God gave the victory!

"A few of the principles and observations, in respect to revival work, which I have learned mainly from our beloved leader, Miss McConnell, I believe it would please the Lord for me to relate now:

"It hardly seems necessary to repeat—holiness is the peak toward which all the other doctrines should focus in revival preaching. Revivals are never preached up, but prayed down. How beautiful it has been to have perfect prayer unity with our sanctified pastors, and thus to see the devil routed. 'If two of you shall agree on earth as touching any thing . . . it shall be done . . .' Matt. 18: 19. When perfect agreement prevails as touching all things related to the revival, namely, the calling, the preaching, the singing, the daily schedule in the parsonage, or whatever else concerns the revival, then God gives the increase without fail. While Brother and Sister

DesJardins pastored the Bryant's Creek church some ten years ago, the preceding verse was thus quickened to all of our hearts. Some of the fruit of that gracious revival remains today.

"Our belief that a revival is a family affair has brought great freedom and released Holy Ghost power in many of our meetings. The first revival held at Index proved the effectiveness of this fact. The missionary family united in prayer. The praying became so intense that at times the pastors while at the schoolhouse about a half mile away, were heard by the evangelist at home in the parsonage, and the pastors testified the same about the evangelist. Heaven suffered violence and the violent took it by force. Our prayers prevailed. A goodly number were saved and sanctified. Some of the pillars of the church there today came out of that first revival, some have moved into other communities, and some are now housed safely in heaven.

"The question is often asked, 'Does it pay?' Our observation on Devil's Creek surely answers 'Yes!' In the first revival on the creek some twenty-eight men, women, and young people were saved, and most of them were sanctified. God gave a glorious meeting. After seven years of further missionary work on the creek, it fell to my lot to go for a second revival effort. We proved the Word of God to be 'quick and powerful and sharper than any two-edged sword.' The battle required this very kind of equipment. Along with the immediate victories, we were blessed over the fact that after seven years

some twenty-two out of the first revival were still
marching onward in the Canaan Land experience.
Added to this victory was the blessed fact that about
ten young people had received calls from the Lord
and are in active Christian service today. I leave the
reader to answer the question, 'Did it pay?'

"It is wholesome always to remember that any revival is the fruit not only of present prayer and
preaching, but it is a result of the accumulated ministry of all the preceding years. Accordingly, after
the years of struggle in our Consolation pastorate,
God gave us the joy of observing the tide turn for
holiness. In this particular revival, one of the best
women in the community finally saw the truth and
became convinced that there is a second definite
work of grace. She immediately began seeking it
like one who long had heard the doctrine; and she
soon found the glorious experience. This victory
stirred the the whole community. Many others followed her into the kingdom. Yes, it was a powerful
revival, but I wonder how far back through the
years its taproot could be traced. One plants, another waters, but God gives the increase.

"Through all the revivals I have experienced during our work in the hills, there has been almost every
kind of devil-incited opposition to overcome early in
our work. But God gave me a verse which up to that
time I did not know was in the Bible. It was my
source of encouragement and power, my rebuke
when tempted to shrink in the battle, and my safeguard when victory crowned the fight. It became

my life verse: 'For it is not ye . . . but the Holy Ghost.' Mark 13: 11.

"In 1931, after the prayerful decision of the executive committee, a Bible School was planned. It fell to my lot to be the one to take up the new burden. The school was four miles from headquarters. Miss McConnell walked the eight miles several days a week to help teach and advise. The knowledge of my utter inexperience for this new task nearly crushed me; but God came to my rescue with this mighty promise, 'The meek will He guide in judgment; and the meek will He teach His way.' Psalm 25: 9. This verse became my meat and drink, and through it, God helped me not to despise the day of small things.

"After the first semester others were added to the faculty. The student body grew. Through much toil our 'white elephant' of a building was converted into a suitable house for the Bible School. Soon a second building was added. Eight years later the flood came! But today God has given, on a new site, more than 'Job's portion' in our present equipment. We praise Him for the many effective holiness workers whom He has sent out from these halls. From the beginning our one consuming aim has been to graduate from this Institute young men and women well settled in the experience and doctrine of true holiness."

One of our circuit riders adds her notes of praise:
"In a broad valley opening on the middle fork of the Kentucky River, has stood the little church and

parsonage for nine years. They are a symbol in the
community of the power and purity of the gospel we
preach.

"For four years I have been privileged to labor
here under the direction of the Holy Spirit. As I look
back over these years and see the victories won, I
marvel at the wonderful grace God has given. His
unfailing Word, with inspired hymns and gospel
songs, has served well to keep me climbing up over
the difficult places. 'With salvation's walls sur-
rounded, I can smile at all my foes,' expresses the
goal for our preaching, for our own lives, and for the
souls in our parish. We have never striven to build
up a large membership of half-way Christians. We
want a people fit to be the spotless Bride of the Lamb.
We praise God for those who have sought and found
the Lord.

"We were early led to press beyond, and hold children's meetings on another creek. The pull became
so strong that a Sunday School developed, then
preaching services, and then a revival of real victories. Our heart's desire was realized when workers were sent there to live and we saw it become a
permanent station; one more lighthouse where souls
can find Jesus.

"From early childhood, I had an ambition to be a
faith missionary. I have found the life far more in-
spirational than depending on a salary. God's checks
are infinitely more reliable than man's. He has
proved Himself an abundant provider. I never
dreamed I would have a fine horse to carry me over

the mountains and through the deep mud, but God gave her to me, thus making our long trips so much easier. 'How beautiful upon the mountains are the feet of him that bringeth good tidings, that publisheth peace.'

"The quiet grandeur of the tree-covered hills charms me. Something of their stedfastness has entered into my soul. 'Far from the madding crowd,' we follow the steps of Jesus seeking the lost sheep."

A faithful pastor and his wife sound their joys which have strengthened their faith:

"God has been gracious to us during these nine years of pastoral work. We have seen many answers to prayer, and nothing has given us more pleasure than to see how God honors His Word and fulfills His promises. We are grateful for every token of His presence. Yes, it warms our hearts when we pause to think on them.

"In the fall of 1937 we began our ministry—our honeymoon being a seventy mile ride to our station. Part of the road was wet and muddy, and we went the last two miles afoot through the rain to our unfinished three-room parsonage.

"Since then we have been puzzled, perplexed, and somewhat depressed at times. On the other hand, we have been surprised and overjoyed as to how God has worked out His will in us and through our pastorate. Personally, He has blessed our souls and supplied our needs beyond our expectations. As we have leaned hard on His promises, and sought to be well acquainted with His Word, we feel that no good thing has been withheld from us because we try to walk uprightly before Him.

"As missionaries our work has been varied; a combination of the regular work of a pastorate coupled with many other types of labor. It is an important matter to be able to use one's hands in manual labor in order to keep the appreciation and respect of the people in this field. We preach in our regular services, at funerals, at memorial meetings held every summer in the family graveyards, in schoolhouses, in homes, and out under the open sky—telling always the gospel of full salvation. Then by calling up and down the creeks and hollows we make contacts not otherwise possible.

"We have found the experience of holiness to be essential in our own lives and in our ministry, and to be exactly what everyone who hungers and thirsts after righteousness needs to satisfy his heart. Those of our people here in this pastorate who enjoy the blessing keep steady, and they quietly and faithfully stay in the narrow way despite every opposition of the enemy. Others seem to come and go as the winds, but with a very few exceptions these sanctified ones remain stedfast and joyful in the faith. As we work with our people, our continual prayer is to be able to present and teach to them this gracious work that God has for all believers. The lives of those who enjoy Holiness are a good witness to the world. It blesses us to see folk with their hearts satisfied and faithfully going about doing God's will."

Sometimes our workers will be asked, "Who is

going to take care of you when you get sick? When you get old what will you do since you do not receive any salary?" Two years ago, the Lord laid it on our hearts to buy a rest cottage, with nice surroundings and eighty acres of land. I was much blessed over this, because it began to be a real concern to me about the care of the workers as the years began to pile up. Somehow I felt this was a pet project of my very own, and so I asked the Lord to pay for it in six months. In a little less than that time, God had sent the entire amount of $4500 to clear the debt.

It is a real joy to know that these faithful, sacrificial men and women can now know that they are going to be well cared for when they retire. The prayer of the Psalmist has already been answered for us, "Cast me not off in the time of old age; forsake me not when my strength faileth." Psalm 71: 9. I have perfect faith for this promise, "They shall still bring forth fruit in old age; they shall be fat and flourishing." Psalm 92: 14, and also for Isaiah 46: 4, "Even to your old age I am he; and even to hoar hairs will I carry you."

———

The many dear children of our pastors and teachers in our K. M. H. A. bring joy and praise, not alone to their parents, but to all of us. We pray that some day God will call them to take up the burdens when some of us who carry them so joyously today, must at last lay them down.

*Little children are remembered in the Saviour's
     promise,*
     *They can early share the blessings of redeem-
       ing grace;*
*He is watching kindly o'er them and His Word as-
     sures us*
     *That in heaven their angels ever see the Father's
     face."*

We love the pioneer missionary work. On and
on we go, carrying the good news into new places.
We have no fear whatsoever but that the Lord will
provide for us all down through our tomorrows.

"Resting and believing, let us onward press,
     *Resting on Himself, 'the Lord our Righteous-
       ness'!*
Resting and rejoicing, let His saved ones sing—
     Glory, glory, glory be to Christ our King!"

We say with Bishop Warren, "Hitherto and Henceforth."

Along with the rich spiritual blessings, the Lord
has given us material blessings as He sees that we
merit or deserve them. At first there was no road
into Mt. Carmel from the highway. Then, in direct
answer to prayer, the county gave us a road. But
to get the things from the road across the Kentucky
River was a problem. A *large swinging bridge* was
constructed fifty feet above the water and three hundred and fifty feet long.

For eighteen years, we have carried tons of goods,

lumber and other things across this swinging bridge which spans the river, then up the steep "Blue Bird Trail" to the school. Finally, we got an old car and made a little truck to back down to the river. This helped much, since after that we need only to carry the things across the river bottom from the road and across the swinging bridge.

Mr. Swauger conceived the idea of stretching a three-quarter inch cable from the campus one hundred feet up in the air over to the road. He hung a large carrier on pulleys. An engine up on the campus pulls the carrier to the campus by a small cable which winds on a cylinder. Surely a God-send to help carry pianos, furniture, cow feed, etc., from the road to the campus on top of Mt. Carmel hill.

Another improvement for which we praise God is the water system which Mr. Swauger, Mr. Paulo, and our boys installed at the headquarters—two deep wells, water-tower and tank, showers and bathrooms, etc. After twenty-one years with no modern conveniences, this added improvement causes us to humbly thank God. This system also affords fire protection which means much to us with our crowded dormitories.

A great source of praise to God came through the fact that of the *hundreds of stars on our service flags,* only a few gold stars appear. Through the lives of some of our boys, the gospel of full salvation was felt in the camps and on the firing lines. Both officers and men often remarked to them about their clean, rich, spiritual lives. Holiness works everywhere.

A certain peculiar richness comes to our hearts from our mountain young people who answer God's call to their own native hills. Some of their testimonies are given here.

Much joy flooded our hearts when *one of our local girls found the Lord*, and then when God called her to preach here in the Kentucky Hills we felt the extra rewards of faith. *Her testimony follows:*

"My soul looks up to God in humility and praise for those whom God called to bring to us the gospel of full salvation. At the age of fifteen, God led me to Mt. Carmel High School. I was clothed in sin and misery, with no joy and no hope. Destruction was my destination. Many times in my life these words formed within my mind, 'Why such a life, nothing to enjoy.' But it was at Mt. Carmel that Jesus revealed the light of salvation to my poor, sin-sick soul. There I saw people singing, shouting, preaching, and most of all *living* the life of holiness. My heart hungered for the joy which they had.

"Sometimes I thought that I must be among the non-elect. One day in girls' prayer meeting, while they were shouting and praising God, I looked up and told the Lord I would do anything for the joy these girls had. I promised Him I would make anything right with man that He showed me. I told Him I was sorry for all the sins I had committed. There swept over my soul a peace, joy, and hope which I had never before experienced. The burden was gone. Jesus had come. Darkness had turned to light. Oh the joy of sins forgiven. I wrote to my folk and told them that I had made a missionary. I told them God had forgiven me for everything. God gave me grace plus blessing as I stood up for Him in my home. He helped me to pray and read the Bible to ungodly loved ones. Two days after God had saved me, He cleansed my heart from sin as the Holy Ghost came in to take up His abode.

"A few months afterward God clearly laid a call upon my heart to preach here in my own native hills. I could not understand things. I told the Lord He had made a mistake by calling a woman to preach. These are the words He whispered, 'Trust in the Lord . . . and lean not unto thine own understanding.' Prov. 3: 5. I began to see what all it would mean to preach two definite works of grace to the people. One day I was startled with this Scripture, 'Woe is unto me if I preach not the gospel.' I Cor. 9: 16. I saw God meant what He said when He told me to preach. Hours were spent in planning on how I would ever get through. I was told by some that I would starve or have to beg if I started out on such a line. So I planned a way through in my mind. I began to look forward to a church, parsonage, garden, chickens and maybe preaching a sermon once a week.

"In my Senior year at high school, while by my bedside praying for the proclamation of God's truth back in the places where they had never heard it, Jesus spoke to my heart these very words, 'I want you to be an evangelistic preacher for me.' All my plans about a garden and chickens disappeared, and all I could see was complete starvation. I began to tell the Lord I could not do it, and beside, what a disgrace that would be for me, a woman. Again the Scripture rang within my ears, 'Woe is unto me if I preach not the gospel.' Other promises such as 'My grace is sufficient for thee' and 'Certainly I will be with thee,' were given to me.

"My experience continued to be up and down until I fully purposed to answer God's call for my life. Thank God for the time when He showed me, through the Word, that it was a Blood-bought privilege and bounden duty of the women, as well as the men, to preach the gospel with the Holy Ghost anointing. I'm thankful for four years at Mt. Carmel High School and for the time He is permitting me to spend here at the Kentucky Mountain Bible Institute, getting the truths of God so that I can go out and be a blessing here in the hills for Him. Thank God, through Jesus, every sin is under the Blood, the carnal nature is gone, and the Holy Spirit abides in my heart. I am going out to spend my life, my all, as an evangelist here in the hills, to help in the spreading of full and free salvation. It seems I cannot find words to express what God has done for me; but this one thing is certain. I expect to answer God's call. I love Jesus with all my heart."

When the Lord lays His hand upon young men to help us in the maintenance work of the Association, our hearts rejoice greatly. This phase of the work is exceedingly important. *A very capable boy who is gifted along this line gives here his account of*

*God's leadings in opening the way for him to come
to Mt. Carmel:*

"I am thankful for the call God has given me. I
count it a joy and privilege to be able to give my life
for Jesus here in the hills of Kentucky. I have had
an unusual interest in the K. M. H. A. from the time
I first heard of the work. It was through my oldest
brother that I first heard of it.

"During the fall revival in my home church that
year, 1938, I went up and gave my hand to the
preacher each night from the beginning to the end.
I didn't get saved, but my heart was hungry for salvation. I was sick of the life I was living. I wanted
somehow to get away from it all. Outwardly, I have
been all right. I don't remember ever taking the
Lord's name in vain. I never tasted whiskey or beer.
I never had the tobacco habit and never bought any
for my own consumption. When I was thirteen years
old, I settled that question, and from that time it has
been, 'No thank you, I don't smoke.' Ninety per cent
of the answers I got from these words proves to me
that I made a good choice. These things were not
from my own goodness; they were the result of the
fact that I had a good father and mother, the kind
that believe that a little soap and water is good for
the mouth when evil words are spoken. I wanted
someone to help me find God, but no one seemed to
be able to do so.

"I was one happy boy when I found out that I
could go to Mt. Carmel. There would be only two
weeks or less till the second semester, but I started

getting ready. I sold a cow that belonged to me and
bought a suit. While I was getting ready mother
tried to get me to put off going until the beginning
of the next school year. Dad didn't want me to go at
all, but said he would not stand in my way if that
was what I wanted to do. He said that he could not
help me any. I knew that some day I would have to
go out and be on my own, and so I decided it might
as well be now as later. For each obstacle that came
up to hinder me from getting to Mt. Carmel, there
came a way to overcome. I didn't have money
enough to buy a bus ticket, but I said I could hitch-
hike. I had no money to pay my school bill, but my
brother had said that I could work and pay it off.

"I was still in sin, but I wasn't happy. I was miserable. And it seemed to get worse all the time. The
Lord saw that I wanted salvation and led me to a
place where I could get help. I am glad for the faithfulness of the Holy Ghost in dealing with me. It took
me a long time to confess out my sins, and to come
to the place where I was willing to give my life in the
hills of Kentucky where God had called me. It
wasn't until April 1, 1942 that I really struck the
solid rock. The Lord Jesus met my soul's need. All
my sins were put under the Blood. Ten days later
came a complete surrendering. I settled the question forever. The Lord put a fixed purpose in my
soul. Full salvation is mine today. I have a joy, a
peace, and a satisfaction that Jesus is mine and that
I am His. I want to live and work that others may
find this salvation.

"The Lord held me steady through three years of army life and let my call grow richer and deeper. Now I am in Bible School, training for the place God has for me. I feel that I of myself can't do much, and the task is large; but the way is upward and forward. 'I can do all things through Christ which strengthenth me.' Phil. 4:13."

A young woman felt the call of God upon her life to the Hills of her own state three years before she entered our Mt. Carmel High School. Her rich testimony, which follows, causes us to praise the Lord and exalt Him:

"Words fail me when I try to express what these past six years in the K.M.H.A. have meant to me. Ever since I came to Mt. Carmel I have heard Miss McConnell and the faithful faculty pray, 'Lord, send the students to our schools whom Thou dost want here; those with hungry hearts who will mind God.' I felt that God answered their prayers when He looked down in Western Kentucky and spoke to my soul. I was the youngest of thirteen children. Ever since I can remember, my heart was longing for God. I did not know how to get saved, and nothing about sanctification; but I was like the Philippian jailor, whose heart was hungry for the Lord, and God led him to the right source. So God led me to His people who had the fire of the Holy Ghost burning in their souls. I praise Him that He ever got me in with the holiness crowd, those who believe in hewing to the line, confessing their sins and praying through to real soul victory.

"After Jesus saved me, I found a need yet in my heart. At times pride, jealousy, and grudge, which is a common trait among us Kentuckians, and many other traits bothered me. One night after hearing a sermon on Hebrews 13:12, 'Wherefore Jesus also, that he might sanctify His people with His own blood, suffered without the gate,' God touched my heart. Later the Holy Ghost burned out carnality and came in to abide.

"In the fall of 1940 Jesus led me to Mt. Carmel High School. I did not have anyone to stand back of me as far as finances were concerned, but I knew I had a great God. Jesus gave me the promise for life in Matthew 6:33, 'But seek ye first the kingdom of God and His righteousness, and all these things shall be added unto you.' He has proved this over and over.

"In my Senior year at Mt. Carmel, Miss McConnell told me she was going to turn me loose in my own native hills for the summer. She sent me to an outstation. This community had been without the gospel. Before I went, the Lord gave me a promise from Isaiah 55:12: 'For ye shall go out with joy, and be led forth with peace, the mountains and hills shall break forth before you into singing, and all the trees shall clap their hands.' We had a good summer there. There were some hard things, but the hardest for me to face were the snakes and lizards. Our house had been used for a corn crib and was well inhabited. The snakes could easily crawl through the cracks in the floor. At night, in my imagination, I could feel a

snake crawling up by my side. I would pray, and
Jesus would give me some good promise. Immediately the devil would try to get me not to believe.
I would then ask the Lord to give me sense enough
to stand on the promise. He would come with fresh
assurance and I would soon go to sleep.

"That fall, the Lord led me to the Kentucky Mountain Bible Institute. These two years here studying
God's Word, under the influence of a godly faculty,
have meant more to me than I can express. I will
never get away from some of the things we are taught
from the Word.

"Jesus has given me a life call here to my own native hills. The call is burning! The command is go!
The fields are white! This is not drudgery, but a
privilege; a God-given privilege!"

The testimony of our young people, when sealed
to their own hearts with unctious overflow blessings,
is a mighty source of praise to our faithful faculty.
*One of our fine mountain lads tells about the Lord's
dealings in his life:*

"When I was very young God dealt with me, and
I felt that I had a call to preach. I did not know the
full meaning of this, but felt the responsibility for
my own people. I never told anybody about my call,
and tried to get away from it because I felt I could
qualify better for something else. I attended a
nearby high school for almost three years. God still
had His hand upon my life, but His overruling providence led me out to what I thought the end of my

school days. But such was not the case. Indeed it
proved to be only the beginning of good things in
my life; for not long after that time I visited Mt.
Carmel with a missionary. It was on a Wednesday
when we came and that night there was a prayer and
praise service. When I heard the young people
praising the Lord and witnessing to His blessing and
keeping power, it made me hungry. That night I
lay awake later than usual. I saw a boy read and
then kneel in prayer, and oh how my heart longed
for freedom from the things that bound me. If I
could only get to the place where my heart didn't
condemn me, I would be happy. I longed for a clear
conscience and a clean heart.

"The next morning there was a good chapel service. Many knew I was under conviction, but I did not
move. Miss McConnell mentioned to the boys that
she hoped I would come to Mt. Carmel and that
maybe I would get saved and God would give me a
call to preach. I had tried for a long time to keep
that call a secret.

"I worked at home that summer and came to
school in September. On September 18, 1941 I was
in a service and it was there that I prayed through.
I had a black record, and it was hard to face people
in making restitution and begging their forgiveness.
But God helped me and I came through rejoicing.

"Two weeks later I saw my need of holiness. I had
not exactly favored it up to that time, but I saw it
then and found myself hungry for it and seeking it.
One of the hardest things I ever had to do was to be

willing to preach. I would do many other things as a Christian, but somebody else could preach. I found out that I had to go God's way, and when I was willing and finally said yes with all my heart, carnality was gone and the Holy Ghost came in. A strange thing happened. I began to love my call above everything that I had planned or kept in reserve. As I witnessed to a call to preach, God blessed me. Others saw their prayers answered for me and were happy with me.

"My life had been warped, and so I had a hard time getting settled because the enemy was always on hand. I came to the camp meeting at Mt. Carmel and while I was there I got my call to the army. I could not understand it all, but trusted God to take me through; not only to protect me from danger and bodily harm, but to keep my heart pure and above sin.

"Today I am back at Mt. Carmel, after two and a half years in active service in the European theater of war. I am rejoicing in His goodness and keeping power. I am thankful that He has brought me back to answer my call to preach in the Kentucky mountains. I do love the Lord today with all my heart and will continue to be what He has intended me to be. I have much to praise Him for."

———————

A young man who was called into the ministry after he was married writes:

" 'Now the Lord had said to Abram, Get thee out of thy country, and from thy kindred, and from thy

father's house, unto a land that I will show thee.'
Gen. 12: 1.

"Having been taught from my childhood days by
godly parents to be obedient, I recognized and answered the voice of the Lord speaking to my heart.
Being a married man, my family must be considered.
We were obedient to our call and God said, 'I will
shew thee whereunto thou must go.' There was a
struggle with Satan when we considered leaving kin
folk and loved ones, and another struggle when we
came to part with the earthly treasures of this world.
Praise the Lord for the sword of the Spirit which we
have in our possession. Luke 12: 15, 'And he said
unto them, Take heed, and beware of covetousness:
for a man's life consisteth not in the abundance of
the things which he possesseth.'

"Satan fled for a season. The Lord knew our need
for more schooling and preparation for our call into
the sacred ministry. We were divinely guided to Mt.
Carmel School through some faithful servants of the
Lord. In spite of all the hindrances to our coming,
we are supremely happy in the will of the Lord. We
have learned to walk closer to Jesus and to enjoy the
fellowship with Him and with His people who also
have been called and are faithful. We are glad for
this good way of holiness. It satisfies our hearts' desires."

One of our dear trustees adds her note of praise:
"I first joined the church and was baptized, but
that did not satisfy me. Then one time I heard Miss
McConnell preach holiness at White Oak and I

Graduating Classes—1946

said, 'That is what my heart longs for.' Time passed but I never got the blessing until after they built Mt. Carmel.

"I truly believed the Lord let affliction come on me in order to make me what He wanted me to be. After Mt. Carmel was built I was sick, and I went off to take treatment. Still I was not well.

"I went to camp meeting one Sunday morning and the children asked me that day when I came back if I was going to church that night. I said, 'Yes, I am going to church, and I am going to the altar, and I mean to stay there all night until I get what the Lord has for me.' They sang a song, 'Nothing between my soul and my Saviour.' The song stayed with me and I said I would have that blessing.

"That night I came across the swinging bridge to church, for I live right across the river from Mt. Carmel. On I went, up the big hill alone in the dark to the service. The song kept ringing in my soul, 'Nothing between my soul and my Saviour.' Someone had said to me when I left the service in the morning that there might be a lot of souls lost if I did not go on and get sanctified. I said, 'I don't want anybody to be lost because of me.' When I came into the chapel one of the teachers asked me if I was going to get sanctified that night. I said, 'Yes, I am getting ripe and ready.'

"I don't remember what Brother Weaver preached about. I sat in the aisle and waited patiently for the altar call to be given. I got up and started to the altar. I just lifted my hands up and said, 'There is not going to be anything between my soul and the Saviour,' and praise the Lord the blessing fell. The Lord sanctified me on the way to the altar. They all knew I had the blessing. I shouted all over the house. I did not care for the world to know it. I said, 'The blessing is so good I want everybody to have it.' I went all over the house. About three days later the Lord healed me.

"The children did not want me to shout. They said, 'Mother, we will not go to church tonight if you are going to shout.' I said, 'Well, I won't if I can help it.' I asked the Lord not to let me shout, but to keep me calm and He did. Praise His holy name!

"When I got the blessing my home did not seem like it did. The birds sang better. The children were different. I said, 'Children, if I stay this happy I never can work any more.' These eighteen years since the Lord sanctified me, Mt. Carmel has been a great blessing to me. I still have the blessing. Praise His name! I have many trials. I feel sometimes I fall short, but God knows my heart and I have no desire to do anything that will be displeasing to Him. I love Him with my whole heart."

———————

The testimony of one of our dear converts follows:
"As far back as I can remember I wanted to be good. I am so glad my parents started me to Sunday School when I was only a small child. I can remember yet going on hot summer Sunday afternoons to the now extinct Maxey schoolhouse where my father and others had Sunday School. The teacher of

the card class, which I was in at that time, was Mrs. Wilus Henry, the mother of Dr. O. P. Henry of Mt. Sterling, Kentucky.

"My father was sick a number of years before he died, and as we children used to go to church and Sunday School mother would stay with him. We were always asked to be able to tell where the preacher took his text and of some of the things he said. Since I was the oldest child this responsibility was mostly mine. Sometimes I would forget. Then father would rebuke me. The next time we started he would say, 'Now children, you listen to the Word and to the preacher better today.' So even when a child the Word meant much to me. I remember the first holiness message I ever heard—it sounded like a strange language.

"When Miss Archer of the K. M. H. A. first preached in our community in 1928, she read the 13th chapter of First Corinthians and talked about perfect love; said that meant being sanctified or having a clean heart. I came home and told mother that that woman preached a new doctrine and told her what Scripture she preached from. Mother said that was not new and, 'That is what your grandfather and grandmother Henry believed.' I knew that they were old-fashioned Methodist people. Their house was always headquarters for circuit riders, and sometimes they had class meetings and other services in their home.

"When I was about twelve or fourteen years old, there had been a revival in our community. One

night the Lord dealt with my heart. Other girls were
going to the altar; I went and prayed some. Someone
helping at the altar came around and said, 'Stand up
and say you are saved.' The other girls did, so I did.
But my heart was never satisfied.

"When Miss McConnell sent people to our community to preach holiness they dealt with me very
carefully, but I still held on to my profession. So I
sought to be sanctified and thought I received the
blessing, but was only saved. No one ever gets sanctified first, or at the same time he is converted.

"It did not take me long to find out that I did not
have in my heart what others had. I grew discouraged, let up in my prayer life, got careless about going to church, and pretty soon quit going and lost
out completely. Folk who have never lost out in
their soul do not know the agony and misery a back-
slider suffers. But the Lord was faithful to follow
after me and convict my heart. At the same time
Christians were praying.

"In May, 1940, Miss Archer held a revival in our
church at Index. The Lord dealt with me and convicted my heart. I will not forget that Sunday morning, May 24. I do not know one thing Miss Archer
said, where the text was found, or anything else, but
I do know what God said. I was to mind Him then
or never. I had been fooling around long enough. I
sought the Lord, confessed every sin, and as fast as
things would come before me I said, 'Yes, Lord, I
will straighten that out.' The Lord wonderfully
saved me. I felt so different, everything and every-

body looked different. Old things had passed away.
All things had become new for me in Christ.

"Now by this time, I knew that in order to live a
clean life one must be sanctified and have carnality
taken out of his heart, that thing that made us want
to sin in the first place. I promised the Lord if He
would save me that the very first opportunity I had
I would seek Him publicly to be sanctified. I prayed
much about it that Sunday afternoon. Satan was on
hand to tell me it was not possible to live without sin.
Then he said no one would want sanctified people
to work for them; and several other things of which
I have found none to be true.

"That same night when the altar call was made, I
went; sought the Lord for a clean heart, put everything on the altar, even to myself. The Lord sanctified me wholly and I have been rejoicing ever since
in His love. The very fact of knowing my sins are
forgiven and carnality gone, blesses my soul yet. I
am rejoicing in this good way of full salvation. I am
becoming more and more excited about it every day.
It is growing on me. It is getting better all the time.

"I promised the Lord I would do anything He told
me to do and He showed me several things. I had to
go to a number of people and straighten out things;
write letters to others. The Lord gave me grace, for
I could not have done all that without His help. But
the blessing and peace that came with it! I would
go home feeling so good because I had another thing
off my soul. I have found much peace and joy in
minding God. The Lord dealt with one woman I

made a confession to, and she asked me to pray with her. Today that woman is saved and sanctified.

"I have never gone hungry as Satan told me I would. I have a good place to work in an office with two doctors in our county seat and have some opportunity to talk to people about their souls. Some patients are sick in their souls and think it to be their bodies. I believe if people would find the Lord that some of their physical ailments would clear up. I do want the Lord to use me every day, every bit He possibly can for His glory.

"Tithing, I have found, helps me to have more money. Sometimes someone says to me, 'Couldn't you use that money for your mother for something?' That tenth belongs to the Lord. I have given nothing unless I give above that. One day out of a clear sky the doctors raised my salary to take care of my tithe. I find when I tithe carefully, and give some offerings besides, the Lord blesses my soul good and gives me more money to give.

"Lately I have been looking around to see what I have given up for Jesus. I can't find a thing. I only exchanged a sinful life for a life of victory, peace and blessing in Him. About a week ago the Lord gave me this promise, Deut. 33: 27, 'God is my refuge.' I need no other. I am believing Him for souls in our community and for my loved ones. I love Him with all my heart. This good salvation satisfies every longing of my soul.

"It blesses me to write this. I pray that it may be a blessing to others who need to know my Jesus."

VII

HINDRANCES TO FAITH

A young man in Northwest Canada, where I had charge of a Bible School, was converted. He came to me after the Lord had truly met his soul in sanctifying power, saying that the enemy was tormenting him. Thoughts of scenes and happenings of his past life would come before him. The devil used this to tell him he was not saved. I told him that this was the enemy's job, to accuse us. In Rev. 12:10, he is called, "the accuser of the brethren." If he belonged to the devil, he would not thus torment him. The devil accuses only the "brethren" or children of God. We cannot prevent the birds from flying over our heads, but we can prevent them from making nests in our hair. Neither can we prevent these thoughts coming to us. Our job is not to harbor them or let them become a part of our thoughts or emotions. Plead the merits of the Blood and the enemy will flee.

Sometimes ugly thoughts and even swear words will come to the Christian. These are not his words; neither does he want them nor say them out loud, but fights against them; consequently, he is not responsible for them. At once the devil will say, "You are backslidden, or these thoughts would not come to you." The suggestion that comes to your mind is no sign that there is sin or carnality present. Eve sinned as soon as she *yielded* to the desire, not when being tempted. Then again, the devil will put horrible dreams on God's people. Beloved, this is no sign that you are backslidden. You have no control over your dreams. However, if folk will keep their minds pure, well-occupied, and stayed on Jesus more, and keep well prayed up, these dreams and thoughts will be less and less frequent. "An idle brain is the devil's workshop."

The enemy will hinder us in our *prayer life* more than in any other one thing. He will let us read the Bible rather than to pray. Prayer is the Christian's safeguard. Prayer accomplishes more than reading or works. The enemy will try to make us feel so busy that we just can't take time to pray. In no other phase of our Christian warfare is he so insistent. He knows that prayer is the secret of the Christian's power and furthermore, the secret of understanding the Word.

When disinclined to pray, of course, this is of Satan. This temptation is to be resisted. We must pray, whether we feel like it or not, as we must do anything else we ought to do. The devil is present always, and never distant. But thank God that He too, Who is stronger than the enemy, is with us all the time. "Ye are of God, little children, and have overcome them: because greater is He that is in you, than he that is in the world." I John. 4:4.

Sometimes the enemy will set siege as he did to Job, but as did Job, we also can keep true to the Lord, and come out *"more than conquerors."* Job 1:22,

"In all this Job sinned not, nor charged God foolishly." Job 42: 12, "So the Lord blessed the latter end of Job more than his beginning."

The Cross has robbed Satan of his power. The devil is a defeated foe. On Calvary, Christ triumphed over the power of darkness. Now, as Christians, we have but to enter into His victory by faith. We do not need to fight Satan, but to hold over him the accomplished triumph of the Cross. Let us live in Ephesians 6 and obey God's commands to "Be strong," "Put on the whole armour of God," "Wrestle," "Stand," "Withstand," "Overcome," "Praying . . . with all perseverence."

Keen says, "The fully saved soul, instead of being free from temptations, is often the subject of the most malignant and persistent attacks of the enemy; but by a steady looking unto Jesus, it is kept on the victory side and can shout with the apostle, 'Now, thanks be unto God, which always causeth us to triumph in Christ.' " II Cor. 2: 14.

Some of God's dear people hinder their influence for the Lord by *majoring on healing.* They have their minds and hearts set on a few Scriptures, and most tenaciously do they hold to these, to the exclusion of deeply spiritual enjoyments such as getting people saved and sanctified. They are driven by a spirit that is unwholesome. There is little fellowship with them. This too, is a trick of the enemy to sidetrack them into this narrow ministry. These dear people are mostly powerless to help folk pray through to forgiveness of their sins, or to drive the enemy away from souls who are seeking to be sanctified.

Of course all of God's people believe in divine healing. Among the rank and file of Christians, many have truly been healed by the Lord. However, the Lord cannot trust some folk with this marvelous blessing, because He knows that they would go off on a tangent about healing, rather than keeping in the middle of the road about it.

I heard Joseph H. Smith relate at a camp meeting in the North, one of his experiences of divine healing. He said, "I was working with another evangelist at a certain camp. The water had affected us so terribly that neither one of us could carry on the work. I said, 'Brother, I'm going to send for a doctor.' The other brother said, 'No, I never take medicine or have a doctor. You will grieve the Spirit if you have a doctor. You must trust the Lord to heal you.' " Brother Smith felt clearly led to send for the doctor. Before the doctor arrived, God had very definitely healed Brother Smith. The other evangelist grew worse. Brother Smith insisted that the doctor examine him. The doctor said, "I have just the very medicine that you need." Finally, after some time, the reluctant evangelist took the medicine and soon was well. God had used this medicine to heal the man. As Brother Smith says, "God won't be dictated to by any of us." That was a clear case of submitting to God's will.

Amanda Smith tells in her autobiography of how the Lord dealt with her concerning divine healing at

one time. On one occasion, this colored evangelist
became very sick. She prayed, but the Lord did not
hear her as He had often done. Amanda had been
mightily used of God in America and around the
world, a powerful preacher of the Word. She
preached on the same platform with men like Joseph
H. Smith, Dr. Carradine, and Dr. H. C. Morrison at
Ocean Grove, N. J., and other places. She preached
at the General Conference in Baltimore, Maryland,
where scores of preachers fell at the altar seeking to
be sanctified under her Holy Ghost-filled messages.
Well, the Lord kept talking to Amanda about getting
a certain kind of medicine. She felt worse and worse.
She said, "Now, Lord, Thou knowest I never take
medicine." Thus the Lord permitted her to suffer
longer, and all the time He kept bringing to her mind
this same medicine. Finally, she consented to send
for the medicine. She took it, and God used it to
help her at once. She said, "Lord, wilt Thou forgive
me, I'll never dictate to Thee again." The Lord grant
unto His people a rich and sane pliableness to His
will. Then our lives and ministry will be much more
effective for His service and glory.

John Wesley says, *"To major on anything but
more love to the Lord, after we are over into Canaan,
is out of divine order and savors of fanaticism."*

Another hindrance to the faith of a Christian,
especially of young Christians, is getting their eyes
on older Christians; on folk who have been in the
way a long time and are more mature in their faith.
Purity is not maturity. Only after we are sanctified

can we grow in grace. However, the perfection of maturity is impossible in this life. That would be a higher standard than in Eden.

Others are hindered because they hide behind what they think are limited possibilities. We know that limited possibilities are not hindrances to perfect union with God. Isa. 35: 8, "And an highway shall be there, and a way, and it shall be called The way of holiness; the unclean shall not pass over it; but it shall be for those: the wayfaring men, though fools, shall not err therein."

A great hindrance to faith and growth in grace is that many *mistake infirmities for sins*. Our mental and physical limitations, since Adam's fall, are indeed infirmities over which we have no control. An infirmity only becomes sin when we detect our error or fault, and then choose to continue in it. No condemnation can exist until we see our fault and are capable of correcting it, and fail to do so. As long as the will is not involved in a wrong choice, there can be no blameworthiness. A holy heart, detecting its error, will admit the error, and abandon it. The discovery that we have been in error does not produce condemnation, but humiliation and regret.

Infirmities come under the law of necessity and are unavoidable. Sins are voluntary. No power on earth can make us sin against our will. Paul tells about his physical infirmities: "Ye know how through infirmity of the flesh I preached the gospel unto you . . ." Gal. 4: 13. "Likewise the Spirit also helpeth our infirmities." Rom. 8: 26. However, with six thousand years of infirmities upon us since Adam's fall, we must watch lest we excuse ourselves from known duty on account of them, and thus encourage self-indulgence. This can have only one end —weakness, and a weak ministry; and perhaps, backsliding. We are commanded, in spite of all our infirmities, to "Be strong in the Lord and in the power of His might." Eph. 6: 10.

Lack of the discernment to understand various situations in Christian work hinders faith. Also, lack of discernment hinders while trying to help folk who are seeking God. Try the spirits. "Beloved, believe not every spirit, but try the spirits whether they are of God: because many false prophets are gone out into the world." I John 4: 1.

Brother John Thompson (Methodist of the Philadelphia Conference and one of the promoters of the holiness movement) was the leader of the Friday Holiness Meeting which met on Arch Street in Philadelphia. A lady who followed one of the modern cults, came in before the service began. She said, "Brother Thompson, I'm to preach here today. God has given me the message." Brother Thompson at once discerned that this was not of God. He said, "Sister, the Lord has laid a message on my heart for today." She kept insisting that she was to preach. Brother Thompson, in his saintly way, said, "Sister, you are out of order." The evil spirit in her soon gave way to impatience, unkindness, and cruel words. The result was that Brother Thompson asked her to leave. She would not. The spirit of the enemy so possessed her that she disturbed the meeting. Finally, Brother Thompson said he would call the officers to take her out. At this she flew into a rage and cursed the preacher while leaving the room. Brother Thompson had learned to "try the spirits."

In our work of faith here in Eastern Kentucky throughout these twenty-two years of holiness ministry, we have striven to *keep all misunderstanding and hindering attitudes cleared up.* This, Beloved, is a great asset to spiritual unity and harmony. We let nothing fester. The early church and the early Methodists used this same method. You will recall that when a misunderstanding arose over the neglecting of the widows in Acts 6: 1, "And in those days, when the number of the disciples was multiplied, there arose a murmuring . . . because their widows were neglected in the daily ministration," the disciples came together and discussed the problem and then prayed. God gave them divine direction just how to proceed until all dissension was entirely cleared up. Acts 6: 2-4. You will see that this pleased the whole crowd. Acts 6: 5, "And the saying pleased the whole multitude." When God speaks, all is well.

Let us endeavor to keep all hindrances to faith and the workings of the Holy Ghost removed, both individually and as a body of Christians. In this way we keep the streams of divine grace surging through our souls. Any grieving of the Lord among the saints, whether in the home, school, church, or in

other religious activities ought to be looked after at
once, so that the work of God be not retarded. Souls
are at stake. Revival fires cannot burn, Christians
cannot become established, young people will not be
able to hear God's call, where there is the grieving
of the Lord through misunderstanding and wrong
attitudes. Matt. 17: 8, "And when they had lifted
up their eyes, they saw no man, save Jesus only."
Peter said, "If ye be reproached for the name of
Christ, happy are ye." I Peter 4: 14.

> *"Only for a moment here,*
> *Heartaches, anguish, pain and tears,*
> *Have their little time.*
> *Soon we'll reach our heavenly home,*
> *Where naught of sorrow ever comes*
> *To mar its blissful clime.*
>
> *Oh, then rejoice! the godly here*
> *Must feel earth's bitterest darts severe*
> *For Jesus felt the same.*
> *There, suffering o'er, with glory crowned,*
> *We'll shout the victory, and sound*
> *Hosannas to His name."*

*Barriers are a great hindrance to personal or
united faith.* If there is the least barrier between you
and any of God's people, there is a very real cause
for it. Either you have sinned or grieved God. It is
only sin that separates us from God or from His people. The only remedy for this is to get back to God,
if we have sinned. God is ever faithful to show us

just what we have done to cause a barrier. Or, if we
have grieved God in any way, by backing down on
something He wants us to do, or have grieved Him
by some actions or words which have not been willful sins (sin is a willful transgression of God's laws),
then we will need to make it right. Whatever the
cause of the Holy Ghost's being grieved, the Spirit is
faithful to reveal to us just what it is. All misunder-
standings need to be ironed out in order for the soul
to be free to trust the Lord, whether for spiritual or
temporal blessings. No one can back down on God's
will and keep saved. *God will not have His religion
mauled around.* He expects us to live so that He
Himself will have confidence in us, and also that
others will have confidence in us. David received
pardon, but he also had to suffer the consequences.

"You stick your neck into a noose when you en-
gage in any habit or practice that is contrary to the
will of God. Sooner or later the devil will draw the
noose. He may not do it immediately. To deceive
you, he may give a little time. He may let you think
for a time that you are getting by. But, sooner or
later, the noose will be drawn, and you will find
yourself in bondage.

"It is dangerous to neglect any of God's commands
or exhortations. The neglect of any of them also
brings one to a state of bondage!"

"Grace is all of God—damnation all of ourselves."
—Keen. Those who are truly spiritual and not under any form of bondage or fanaticism, are so satisfied, for they are enjoying the rich things of the

Conference Group of Kentucky Mountain Holiness Association in session at the Headquarters—Mt. Carmel High School—June, 1946

Cross. Their ministry is always constructive and helpful and brings great glory to Jesus. II Thess. 2: 15, "Therefore, brethren, stand fast, and hold the traditions which ye have been taught, whether by word, or our epistle."

Quoting from *Memorial Papers* by Keen: "There are many preachers today who were once warm, forceful, happy men in the ministry; who, by this process of preaching another gospel, and preaching other preaching, other than that which they have been bidden to preach, have impoverished their own experiences in the things of God. Their souls have run dry. They have no spirit for their work left in them. They are not backslidden, nor dead at heart, but are in spiritual atrophy—starved by their own ministry. One of the ablest, most earnest, and popular pastors in Methodism today has written me recently: 'I have dropped down in my tone. The old themes do not move and fire me. I cannot preach them or feel them as I once did.' A sad victim of a snare of the devil, which has caught many an earnest, godly pastor, and shorn him of his power to save souls! We must return to the old, soul-saving truths, and continue in them; get back to the work of preaching a Holy Ghost gospel and stick to it." Psalm 11: 3, "If the foundations be destroyed, what can the righteous do?"

The preaching of the Word of God in all of its fulness, in all protestant pulpits, in home and foreign lands, would mean a gracious warmth. Soon it would bring about a mighty change of thought and eventually cause millions of people to seek the Lord and find true rest for their souls. Each time, when Israel turned to God, as we find in the book of Judges, she had great success in every way.

> *"How firm a foundation, ye saints of the Lord,*
> *Is laid for your faith in His excellent Word!*
> *What more can He say than to you He hath said,*
> *To you who for refuge to Jesus have fled?"*

The only reason why more than a hundred men and women have applied to be blown up on the Atom Bomb test ships is because they have lost their faith. Most of these are rich and educated. Only God can bring rest and satisfaction to life. When the enemy of souls seeks to pile things upon God's people to discourage, they can quench all his fiery darts by the shield of faith. "Above all, taking the shield of faith, wherewith ye shall be able to quench all the fiery darts of the wicked." Eph. 6:16. Beloved, around the globe this old-time, heart-felt religion works in all lives who truly possess it. It is the only remedy for individual and global conflicts.

Just as the blooming rose will make fragrant the desert waste, man will see in Christ "all power" to transform, purify, and sanctify not only the individual but the whole world. Christlike men believe not only in the sufferings of Christ, but they "fill up the measure of his sufferings" by suffering with Him. "Christ also suffered for us, leaving us an example, that ye should follow his steps." I Peter 2:21. Such men press their way to heaven through loss, persecution, scorn, false brethren, and spiritual foes.

Some Bible facts about sin:

First: —"All unrighteousness is sin." I John 5: 17

Second: —"He that committeth sin is of the devil." I John 3: 8

Third: —"Sin is a trangression of the law." I John 3: 4

Fourth: —"To him, therefore, that knoweth to do good, and doeth it not, to him it is sin." James 4: 17

Fifth: —"In sin did my mother conceive me." Psalm 51: 5

There is no possible "power to become the sons of God" until all sinful choices are abandoned and pardon for the past secured; nor is there any possible power of the Holy Ghost coming upon you in sanctifying power until the sin that dwelleth in you is cleansed away. Putting away and confessing sins must precede sonship; cleansing from all unrighteousness must precede being filled with the Holy Ghost. Empowering is not the remedy for sin; it is the Blood, not Spirit; it is cleansing; not filling. The Blood stands forth as God's remedy for sin; the Holy Ghost is the renewer and sanctifier.

In my first book, *"The Pauline Ministry in the Kentucky Mountains,"* I have devoted part of Chapter Eight to the discussion and remedy of one form of *social sin,* namely, "secret sin, or masturbation." This discussion has proved very helpful to a great number of souls. I have received letters from many troubled hearts thanking me for the vital and definite help that they have received from it. Also, some

distressed souls from different parts of the nation
have come to us for prayer and help. Praise God,
there is a remedy for every troubled soul. The devil
never got a soul into anything but what the Lord
could get him out, and keep him clean, true, happy,
and powerful. We praise God for helping us to thus
write about this very common sin so that souls who
truly wanted help could find it. I quote from a letter
received from a pastor:

"I want you to know I would not trade your book
for any book in my library. It gave me an insight on
the kind of life I have hungered and thirsted after
for so long. God blessed and convicted (mostly convicted) my heart. I have been living a so-called
Christian experience, but not a really rich life of
faith for God. I have never received real joy in my
experience. I received very few blessings from God.

"After reading your book I have finally found out
why. Miss McConnell, this book was written to dig
me out of my lethargy; especially your writing on
the "secret sins." This has been my trouble for
years, even though I have been married for nine
years. I could not keep victory over this. This is
why I have lived an up and down life these many
years.

"After finishing the reading of this book, I deter-
mined to get rid of this trouble and have the song
bird in my soul. At 6: 35 P. M. I went to my knees
and began confession to Jesus and at 7: 20 P. M. Jesus came and spoke peace to my soul. Immediately
I felt I must have the carnal nature removed to live

a victorious life. I went to my knees the second time
and at 9: 20 P. M. I felt the cleansing power of Jesus'
Blood. I claimed the promise, John 1: 7 and I have
victory in my soul. Thanksgiving is in my soul this
morning as I write this letter of appreciation to you.
Again I say, thank you, and of course God, for writing this book."

I came across a very helpful and Scriptural message along the line of socially clean living which I
will give here. It is given by an early Methodist
preacher who was sanctified wholly. I trust it will
be a mighty blessing to many troubled hearts who
are seeking for help along these lines in their social
life. It is a discussion of the *Relation of the Senses
and Appetites and Desires to Holiness.*

"The relation of the physical to the spiritual is one
of the important questions in solving the doctrine of
holiness. The appetites were given to preserve man-
kind individually, the passions to perpetuate the
race; and to pervert either, must lead to countless
evils, whether done ignorantly or intentionally.

"The forbidden things against which holiness
makes its protest are not natural, but unnatural
things; perversities of nature. The senses, passions,
and appetites of our physical life are God-appointed,
and are to be used for the end for which He appointed them, and not to be destroyed or abused.

"Sensuality is utterly incompatible with a holy
heart and life. 'The body is not for fornication, but
for the Lord.' The mind that regards the body as an
instrument of sensuous delights, merely has forgot-

ten Paul said, 'Know ye not that your bodies are the members of Christ?' I Cor. 6: 15, and exist not for the play of their own senses, but as 'instruments of righteousness unto God.' Rom. 6: 13. Many professing to be holy seem to be ignorant of the divine use of the body, and their misuse of it leads others to doubt the reality of their experience. Because of this, many don't believe holiness is obtainable in this life. Abornomal use of our bodies must lead to suffering, disease, and death. Much of the life that now is, is the accidental fruit of misguided appetites and passions, having no end to serve, and mental protest exists against its conception through misuse. The tale of inherited prenatal dispositions toward evil, through ignorance, will never be told. Even holy parents, through ignorance of physical laws and mental influences, may propagate evil by uncontrolled passions, who would shrink from such acts, if they understood the consequences, as they would from a viper in their path. In all these things, Scripture is silent concerning detail, but covers them by a broad principle, 'Whatsoever ye do, do all to the glory of God.'

"James says, 'Each man is tempted when he is drawn away by his own lust and enticed.' If yielded to, then comes SIN. To determine temptation from without, which is compatible with the greatest degree of holiness, and the promptings of sin within us, one must distinguish between a desire awakened by the senses, appetites, and passions, while the inner man recoils from sympathy with such desires, and an inner affinity for evil things, from whatever source they may arise.

"The Saviour has placed lustful desires in the catalogue of adultery in the heart. Of course he means a forbidden desire entertained in the affections. To properly regard the object for which marriage was instituted cannot be lust, for God in the beginning made us so; but a desire to misue the relation, though sustaining the relation of marriage, is born of lust, and it brings forth sin. Thousands of professing Christians are misusing the married relation to serve unholy ends, and defile the relation. A pure bride and bridgroom are God's chosen type of the relation of a pure heart to God. Any act that produces a sense of defilement in the heart of the perpetrator must be an unclean act. There is a crying demand for cleansing from 'all filthiness of the flesh,' and that 'fornication and all uncleanness, . . . let it not be once named among you, as becometh saints . . .' There needs to be an end of so much secret confidence concerning the secret life of the married relation; and surely the ranks of the holy will be advanced when some of its professors cease teaching younger ones how to successfully feed the passions, while they hate the ends for which God gave them. Be clean! Be clean! in every secret sense from all filthiness of the flesh, ought to ring out everywhere, until every act seen of God can meet the divine approval. Holiness demands that we should be true to the laws of our physical life as we understand them, as well as spiritual laws, and much sickness, disease, and death would be averted by a faithful regard for every revelation of truth here as elsewhere.

"Involuntary physical action does not affect our spiritual state. Consent to the misuse of our physical powers demonstrates the existence of wrong motives which are contrary to holiness. Appetites and passions that have been implanted by God are not to be crucified, but controlled; perversities are to be destroyed. We count that desire depraved that seeks a forbidden object. There could be no sinful desires if there were no innocent ones.

"Professor Bowne says, 'the highest act of the free soul is the acceptance of our true nature. Our bodies, being God's temple, should be holy. Novalis said, 'There is but one temple in the world, and that is the body of man.' 'KEEP THYSELF PURE.' "

Many dear folk over the nation have come to the writer for help along spiritual lines. One of the most common burdens of distress of their hearts has been: How can I keep rich in my soul and true to God and have victorious faith and live a normal married life from the married relation standpoint?

Beloved, anything that grieves God and thus lessens our spiritual joys, proves that it is out of divine order. Some folk would rather over-indulge the flesh than have the powerful and clean life for body, mind, and soul. These are always powerless souls and hinder the work of God wherever their lot is cast, even though they still profess to have salvation.

God instituted the sacred laws of marriage; but He will not permit marriage to be a license for lust.

John Wesley says in commenting on the verse, "That every one of you should know how to possess his vessel in sanctification and honour;" I Thes. 4:4 "This requires knowledge as well as chastity so as neither to dishonor God Himself, nor to obstruct, but further holiness; remembering marriage is not designed to inflame, but to conquer natural desires." We quote Wesley's comment on I Thes. 4:3, 5, 6: "In this matter—by violating the bed. The things forbidden here are three: fornication, v. 3; the passion of desire or inordinate affection in the married state, v. 5; and the breach of the marriage contract, v. 6." I Thes. 4:6, "The Lord is the avenger of all these things." Those who are living Scripturally along these lines are supremely happy in the family life, and their children are not cursed by the sins of their parents.

God has never left folk in the dark about anything. Those who put God first are controlled by divine love and thus honor the Holy Ghost. These dear sanctified folk are not living under any nervous strain or any physical torment, but just as God intended married folk to enjoy life.

VIII

FAITHFUL CO—LABORERS

During the first year of my labors in the mountains, God put me to many tests. These strengthened me for all the future trials or hardships, and gave me a good point of contact with the people in the rural sections. It was to these needy, long-neglected communities that the Lord had called me.

I was cold and hungry often during that first long, lone winter. The Lord knows how to prepare us for a deeper, stronger ministry and leadership. Thus He permitted many hard battles to come my way. I thank God for each one of them, not alone because of the victories won in every case, but also because the Lord was getting me ready to help the younger workers that He was beginning to call into this work of Faith.

I believe that God primarily called me *first* into the work, to help establish schools and churches as a direct means of getting the Gospel to the recesses of the mountains. *Second,* He called me to this task so as to lead the way for many other men and women to come in answer to His own calling for their lives. Not alone is the work carried on in their own native hills through the young people that have been trained in our schools, but also through many pastors and teachers whom God has so definitely led into our Kentucky Mountain Holiness Association from many states and from many different denominations.

God has sent into this Home Mission Field a strong and spiritual group of well-qualified men and women to help spread Scriptural holiness. We require every worker to have at least three years of training beyond high school. However, the large majority of our workers have finished their college work and a few have their Master's Degree in Theology. My soul is strengthened and greatly blessed to work with these holy workers.

Holiness moistens its labors with weeping and prayers. "They that sow in tears shall reap in joy. He that goeth forth and weepeth, bearing precious seed, shall doubtless come again with rejoicing, bringing his sheaves with him." Psalm 126: 5, 6. As with Isaiah, only the perfect cleansing from sin will cause us to go anywhere and do any work for the Lord. Isaiah 6: 8, "And I heard the voice of the Lord saying, Whom shall I send, and who will go for us? Then said I, Here am I; send me." Beloved, it is sanctification that fits the believer for all good work. II Timothy 2: 21, "If a man therefore purge himself from these, he shall be a vessel unto honour, sanctified, and meet for the Master's use, and prepared unto every good work." Until filled with the spirit of holiness, religion will always manifest the spirit of self, or compromise, or human policy, or other questionable means of procedure. This hinders faith altogether; so that God cannot work to the salvation of souls or the building up of the saints. Further-

more, holiness brings out the latent powers of the
soul to work for Jesus.

In this spiritual warfare I am often led to exclaim
like Deborah, "O my soul, thou hast trodden down
strength." Judges 5: 21. Through these twenty-two
years, with this corps of well-trained and sanctified
men and women, we have been claiming the promise, "The mountains shall be thine." God said to
Moses, ". . . and they shall bear the burden of the
people with thee, that thou bear it not thyself alone."
Num. 11: 17.

Ephesians 4: 11, 12, "And He gave some apostles;
and some, prophets; and some evangelists; and some
pastors and teachers; For the perfecting of the saints,
for the work of the ministry, for the edifying of the
body of Christ." The Lord has fulfilled this in our
work. He has called some to be preachers, evangelists, pastors, and teachers, all for the perfecting of
the saints, i.e., to get folk saved from their sins and
their hearts cleansed from inbred sin or carnality.
As Paul testified before Agrippa, "Now I send thee,
To open their eyes, and to turn them from darkness
to light, and from the power of Satan unto God, that
they may receive forgiveness of sins, and inheritance
among them which are sanctified by faith that is in
me." Acts 26: 17, 18.

It has been said, and sad to say it has come to pass
in some cases, that when the founder or leader of a
work has gone to his or her reward, that sooner or
later, the work has not kept true to the principles
which it was raised up to promote. Especially, is this

very noticeable in the realm of the spiritual. Why is this so?—only because the future leaders have failed to keep true. God kept the work clean and spiritual for years because the leaders kept true in heart and life, and thus God was honored and wisdom and grace were given to carry on. Just so will He keep any work true as long as folk will pay the price and be true to the precious Word of God.

"As I was with Moses, so I will be with thee: I will not fail thee nor forsake thee." Joshua 1: 5. God is the same yesterday, today, and forever. Deuteronomy 7: 9, "Know therefore that the Lord thy God, He is God, the faithful God, which keepeth the covenant and mercy with them that love Him and keep His commandments to a *thousand generations.*"

Obedience to God's commands will keep and sustain any work of God forever. The warning is found in Deut. 11: 26-28, "Bchold, I set before you this day a blessing and a curse; A blessing, if ye obey the commandments of the Lord your God . . . ; And a curse, if ye will not obey the commandments of the Lord your God, but turn aside out of the way. . . ." "I exhort you," said Moses, "to fully obey the Lord." Deut. 8: 7, 9, "For the Lord thy God bringeth thee into a good land . . A land wherein thou shalt eat bread without scarceness, thou shalt not lack any thing in it. . . ." Our great promise, Josh. 17: 18, will continue to be fulfilled as long as we, like Caleb, wholly follow the Lord. "Meditate upon these things; give thyself wholly to them; that thy profiting may appear to all. Take heed unto thyself and unto the doctrine, continue in them: for in doing this thou shalt both save thyself, and them that hear thee." I Tim. 4: 15, 16.

One of the things that cut deeply into my heart is the fact that sometimes we cannot answer the call of the dear people for workers to some long-neglected community. Just this year (1946) at our June conference, we were unable to answer the urgent calls from five different creeks for a church and Sunday School to be started there.

The Kentucky Mountain Holiness Association is an *interdenominational* work, *incorporated* in 1931. It has meant much to have as *trustees* of this Association a group of men and women who love us and advise us and pray for us. The present board is: Dr. F. H. Larabee, Dr. H. J. Hervey, Dr. Peter Wiseman, Dr. C. W. Butler, Dr. Warren C. McIntire, Mr. James J. Pursell, Mr. C. C. Valade, Miss Minnie Evans, Rev. Lela G. McConnell, Rev. Don A. Morris, Rev. Gene E. Phillips, Rev. Martha L. Archer, Rev. Karl S. Paulo, Mr. R. L. Swauger, Mrs. R. L. Swauger, Dr. W. E. Harrison, Miss Genelle A. Day, Rev. L. O. Florence, Mrs. Blanche Haddox, Mrs. Sam Noble, Rev. Lloyd M. Blakely, Dr. E. R. Overley, Dr. J. C. McPheeters.

I am quoting some of the calls and testimonies of a few of our one hundred pastors, teachers, and helpers. I regret very much that I cannot publish in this short volume something from each one of them.

"When I was a Sophomore in Mt. Carmel High

School, one Wednesday night in prayer meeting the altar was opened for seekers and for those to whom the Lord was talking about a life call. I knew Jesus in His saving and sanctifying power, but found my way to the altar earnestly desiring to know if there could be any place in the Lord's work that I might fill. I fully believed I did not have enough talent, but when He had saved me at the age of twelve I promised to spend my time telling others of Jesus. He laid the burden of my own mountain people upon my heart, and I left the altar fully trusting Jesus to show me clearly.

"The Lord so ordered it that the third chapter of Exodus was given to me for my topic for Young People's Meeting the next Sunday. Down in Classroom A as I prayed about the message, the Lord assured me He was calling me as He did Moses to lead his own people out of Egypt. I was sure I must be mistaken as to the Lord's leadings and told Him, in all earnestness, that I could not preach great sermons like other people, neither could I sing. I was very timid. My heart was aching for my people and I wanted to do something for Him and them. God assured me that He was not asking me to preach great sermons, or to sing, but to tell them the simple story of salvation. Then for my life verse, He gave me Exodus 3:12, 'Certainly I will be with thee; and this shall be a token unto thee, that I have sent thee: ...'

"Then I told the Lord that many did not believe women should preach. For that need, He gave me the same message that He gave Moses, 'I AM hath

sent me unto you.' With quiet but heart-felt consecration, I sang softly:

> *'There is surely somewhere a lowly place*
> *In earth's harvest field so wide*
> *Where I may labor through life's short day,*
> *For Jesus the crucified.*

> *'I'll go where you want me to go, dear Lord,*
> *Over mountain or plain or sea.'*

"The word mountain was so large that I could
hardly sing any further. As I paused, waves of blessing swept over my soul in sweet assurance that I had
found the Lord's place for my whole life. Then He
gave me a vision of little white churches, old schoolhouses, large congregations of mountain people sitting with hungry hearts and bowed heads, waiting
for me. I was coming toward them with a suitcase in
each hand. The vision attended by His promise to be
with me caused me to sing:

> *'So trusting my all to Thy tender care,*
> *And knowing Thou lovest me;*
> *I'll do Thy will with a heart sincere,*
> *I'll be what you want me to be.'*

"Literally my call and vision have been fulfilled.
I have had the privilege of carrying my suitcase
many times as well as other things, and walking
many miles. I have preached in Kentucky Mountain
Holiness Association churches, schoolhouses, and
have been the first to preach full salvation to some.

"Times without number my co-worker and I climbed a very steep hill to pray with a sick lady who was not sanctified. At last when she was almost too weak to speak, the blessing came and we knew it as soon as we stepped into the room. As we sang 'The Hallelujah Side' she waved her weak hand in praise to the lovely Christ who had sanctified her heart. No matter how long the trip, it could not be a task when a hungry soul is at the other end.

"Another young girl and I were sent to open a station one summer. Knowing the place, I asked for an older co-worker, but there was no one to send except a younger girl who was less experienced than I. Realizing we knew so little about station work, I asked for wisdom, sense, understanding, and the physical strength of ten women. He gave us so much of Himself that our hearts greatly rejoiced in Him. We moved into an old house which we had to clean, scrub, disinfect, and paper.

"When I became a permanent worker I reminded the Lord that He had called me, even though I felt incapable. I was His preacher and must have a holiness library. While I prayed, the Lord spoke to a sanctified man in Detroit, Michigan and the many good books which he has sent have been a great asset to my ministry.

"Surely God has been with me and this has been a token that He sent me. Truly, 'The steps of a good man are ordered by the Lord, and he delighteth in His way.' Psalm 37: 23. 'In all thy ways acknowledge him, and he shall direct thy paths.' " Prov. 3: 6.

"I went to Bible College in the North four years
and received a head knowledge of salvation, but as
far as making its joys experientially mine, that day
never came. I sought the Lord from time to time,
but my deepest need was never met because I never
fully uncovered the carnal traits that were causing
me so much trouble. I would pray about them, even
worry about them. Meanwhile, the enemy of my
soul would suggest, from time to time, that God was
not able for my case, for I was hopeless. However,
I kept on professing and doing the best I could to live
a clean life, trying to forget my failures, and to serve
the Lord in any way I could.

"It was while I was still in this weak spiritual state
that the Lord spoke to my heart about working for
Him in the hills of Kentucky. He definitely spoke to
me through Acts 26: 16-18 and I knew it was His
voice calling me to the hills. From childhood, I had
been told of the heartache and strife that often comes
from not minding God, and at this particular time
it was that early training which wonderfully helped
me to choose God's way in the face of opposition.

"Once in the hills, the word holiness took on an
entirely new meaning. The people here talked about
it more than I had been used to. They seemed to get
great joy and blessing out of testifying about how the
Lord had sanctified them and set them free from the
carnal nature. How the Lord did honor such testimonies!

"The first thing which the Lord began to reveal to
me was the depth of the stain of sin in my own heart

and life. It was going to take more than a few minutes of praying around some altar to straighten out
what sin had woven into my very nature. But realizing my need, the Lord helped me to face the issue
just as it was. Hard as it was, I was made to see, for
the first time, that if I ever won through to complete
victory over self and sin, I was going to have to confess those carnal traits which had hounded me day
and night for so long.

"About this time the Lord knew I needed some
encouragement, and so He gave me the promise, 'Sin
shall not have dominion over you.' Rom. 6: 14. How
gracious was this promise to my heart, after being up
and down for so long. My eyes were opened to the
efficacy of the Blood to cleanse my heart from all sin.
I had never realized so fully before that the Blood
has such far-reaching extent of power to save and
sanctify.

"Since the day I settled it to go clear through,
Psalm 84: 11 has been mine continually. I praise God
that I have found an experience in grace that really
works. I am His and He is mine."

"When my wife and I finished our college work,
we began to look about for a place of service. However, we had drifted far from true holiness, and
while we still moved in the general direction of God's
call, that call had become the excuse for personal
ambition. Money, honor, position—these were more
in our thoughts than true service to God and to souls.

"When, through corresponding with friends at the

Kentucky Mountain Bible Institute, we began to realize that God was calling us to Kentucky, we were not altogether happy to go where so little money or prestige was to be gained. However, we felt so definitely that God wanted us in the K. M. H. A. that I quit a good job; we refused other offers, and prepared to make the trip. We comforted ourselves with the plan of staying only a short time, unless things should be to our liking.

"On arriving at K. M. H. A. at camp meeting time, we were moved by conflicting feelings. The educational standards of the schools, the gifts and graces of the workers, made us congratulate ourselves that we had found so choice a place. From the moment that we stepped on Mt. Carmel campus, we felt, 'This is home!' God was there, and this was His place for us.

"However, we had little success in attempting to fit into the spiritual atmosphere, for the constant emphasis on genuine Scriptural holiness, and the evident blessing of God on others, made us uneasy in the growing consciousness of our own emptiness.

"We found that others were praying at the altar to be forgiven for sins which we had been excusing in ourselves. We began to lose our appetite and to lie awake nights; still we resented the suggestion kindly made that we might have a spiritual need. We sat back to pick flaws in the preaching, knowing something surely must be wrong here, because we felt so queer. Of course, it could not be in ourselves.

"When we finally discovered that many were

deeply concerned for our souls, we went alone to pray, and God gave us grace to be honest. The Lord convinced us as no man could do, of our backslidden state.

"Shocked and dazed at the revelation of our own hearts, we groped painfully to get back to the light. Weeks of floundering passed before we could fully recognize and obey the voice of God. When finally we said 'yes' to God's call (which we had unconsciously been unwilling to admit), and covenanted to stay in the K. M. H. A. and take the humble place, the burden lifted and light came into our souls.

"A week later the Lord enabled us to see and confess the pride and selfishness and ambition of our hearts, and we consciously gave ourselves to Him to be 'sanctified, and made meet for the Master's use,' in humble service.

"Sometimes we wondered during those days of bewildered seeking, why we must take such a stumbling, long-drawn-out way to get to God; but many times since then we have been thankful for every lesson learned, and for the settling of things back there; for it has not only held us steady in times of great pressure, but has also given us an insight into the needs and problems of others, and helped us to understand how to point them to God.

"Life is new again. Salvation is not feeling, but consciousness. Holiness is not a doctrine, but a blessed experience. Preaching is not the expression of a beautiful sentiment, but the delivery of a message. God is real. The Bible preaches to us. The

cynicism and futility of the past are gone. 'We're in
the land of Canaan, abundantly satisfied.' Praise the
Lord."

"My heart is full of praise as I remember the marvelous works that He has done in my own life. First
of all, I thank Him for picking me up out of a stiff,
formal, Presbyterian church in a western town in
Canada and saving my soul. I had been taught that
I had to sin more or less every day. Also, I praise
Him for showing me that I could be sanctified, get rid
of all sin, be free from carnality, and have the presence of the Holy Ghost in all His fullness in my heart.
I thank Him that I received power to witness and live
a pure, holy life in the face of much opposition from
home and worldly church members.

"A year later I felt the Lord was leading me into
Christian work. I knew not what, nor where. He
wonderfully opened the way for me to go to the Chicago Evangelistic Institute, the holiness school of His
choosing. Shortly before graduation, Miss McConnell gave us a stirring message as to the needs in the
mountains. It took hold of my heart, but I wanted to
be absolutely sure it was the Lord's leadings, so I
asked Him for a verse to stand upon. This is the
Word He quickened to my heart, 'Then the eleven
disciples went away into Galilee into a mountain
where Jesus had appointed them.' Matt. 28: 16. All I
could hear was God's appointment for me to the
mountains.

"These eight years living by faith, doing His will,

standing on the promises, have been the best years of my life. My heart has been made to rejoice again and again, as I have seen souls saved and sanctified in revivals and in the homes and have seen them 'serve Him without fear in holiness and righteousness.'

"Oh, the joy it brings to be in the center of His will, to be co-workers with Him, proving this verse continually: 'God is able to make all grace abound toward you that ye, always having all sufficiency in all things, may abound to every good work.' II Cor. 9: 8.

"I can't begin to praise the Lord enough for supplying all my needs spiritually and temporally. Truly He has done exceeding abundantly above all I could ask or think. Holiness really works in my life and I can say with Paul, 'Thanks be unto God which always causeth us to triumph in Christ.' II Cor. 2: 14. I count it a privilege to have a little part in the triumph of holiness in the Kentucky Mountains."

"All during my childhood days my heart was inclined toward spiritual things, and thus I was hungry for God's leadings. Miss McConnell came to her home church, which is also my home church, and told of the work God had led her to establish in the mountains of Kentucky.

"On one of the circulars which portrayed the work, under the needs of the work, the words 'Consecrated workers' made a lasting impression on me. I carried the circulars in my purse, and while riding

to and from the office where I worked, I would take
them out again and again and study them. Through
this and other influences, the feeling that I should go
to the mountains was increasingly impressed on my
heart. One day while working in the office in Philadelphia, Pa., I wrote these lines:

A longing to work in the mountains
Is pondered down deep in my heart;
Its vision is ever before me,
And from me shall never depart.

I knew nothing of what it meant to be called of God
to some special work, but there was a deep yearning
in my heart to walk in the little light I had.

"Despite the opposition of many folk, my own ti-
midity, and lack of funds, preparations were made,
and in a short time I was enrolled as a student in the
Kentucky Mountain Bible Institute, there to lay a
good foundation physically, mentally, and spiritually for the work to which God had called me.

"The mighty power of the Holy Ghost upon the
faculty and students of the Bible School, and their
sincere, unctious testimonies convinced me that they
possessed something real in their hearts for which I
had been seeking for a long time. Just one week
after entering school I found the Lord in saving
grace. Then as the light dawned in upon my heart,
I began seeking earnestly for holiness. After confessing out the carnal nature and fully consecrating
my all to Jesus, the Holy Ghost came in His cleansing
power, eradicating inbred sin and took full posses-

sion of my soul. I now had the initial equipment to
answer God's call. What a marvelous change had
come into my life! While meditating on this great
contrast, the Lord gave me these lines:

> *Jesus saw me as I sat in darkness,*
> *Plunged beneath the awful shame*
> *That of sin and its allurements,*
> *Now, I'm free, Oh praise His name.*

> *Praise His name the light now shineth,*
> *Darkness, yes, has taken flight;*
> *Jesus has in all His fullness*
> *Turned my darkness into light.*

> *Glorious light! ay yes I find it,*
> *Yet I hear Him as of yore,*
> *As to the just He speaketh*
> *Your path, it shineth more and more.*

"When the Lord began talking to me about the
mountains, little did I realize the tremendous need;
nor did I know of the hard situations to be faced. On
the other hand, I had no idea of the deep satisfaction, the abiding contentment, and supreme delight
that would be mine in fulfilling God's call in a work
of faith. Truly, 'The lines are fallen unto me in
pleasant places.'

"Through these years God has wonderfully supplied my every need; has given me a good sanctified
husband and two lovely children; and in some experiences almost beyond human endurance He has

fulfilled His Word, 'We went through fire and water, but Thou broughtest us out into a wealthy place.' Psalm 66: 12.

"During each of the thirteen years I have been here, there has come an unfolding of God's purpose in establishing this holiness center in the hills of Kentucky. In every phase of the work the evangelists, pastors, teachers, and helpers are working together in the unity of the Spirit, not only for the salvation of precious souls, but also for the saving of 'lives' that they may be trained to herald the gospel of full salvation around the world.

"There is deep gratitude in my heart for the divine call to labor here; for the rich, vital training received in the Bible School and further training in Asbury College; and the divine enduement to perform that which God has called me to do."

"From the time I was a small child, my heart had been hungry for God. I cannot remember the time when I did not want to do His will and serve Him. At an early age I promised God that as soon as I was old enough I would join the church and be baptized. This would mean I would give the preacher my hand and be immersed, without any change of heart or life. It was all I knew to do to follow God. When I was older I felt that this step would not satisfy my heart. I saw how others had followed that method but they did not show any signs of real salvation.

"During the fall of 1935, I was deeply under conviction. God was talking to me and pleading with me about my soul. For a period of time, I did not care for food, and often went to school without any dinner. I was so hungry for God I wrote to my older sister who was in school at Mt. Carmel, asking her to pray for me to get saved. I knew she would pray for me because she had been saved at school. I prayed, but not knowing how to pray or seek God, I did not get saved at that time.

"In direct answer to prayer, three missionaries came from Mt. Carmel to our community in the summer of 1936. I was visiting our nearest neighbor when they arrived in an old car, with a trailer full of supplies hitched on behind. I well remember my feelings and desires. I ran into the house to hide my bare feet as they passed by, going to my home. They came to live in a log house belonging to my married sister who is now walking with God.

"They planned to preach and teach Sunday School in the schoolhouse. The superintendent would not give his permission, as he feared the window lights would be broken out during the services. But the missionaries prayed, knowing God had led them there for the summer. Not far from their little house was an unoccupied house that had been used for storing fodder. It was unfinished, with the partition taken out between two of the rooms. Thus it made enough space for a good-sized congregation. There were no seats or a pulpit. One of the girls made a nice little pulpit from a plank. Then they rolled stones down from the hillsides and laid planks across them for seats. The seats were not very comfortable

because they were so low. This was not a place of
comfort and beauty, but a place where God blessed.
Eternity alone will tell of the truth that went home
to darkened hearts in that crude 'chapel.' There
the gospel in its fullness was preached to many hearts
for the first time.

"After making personal calls in the homes and
praying with the people, the missionaries felt it was
God's time for a revival. A lady evangelist from Mt.
Carmel came and began holding services each night.
They had a prayer meeting in some home each morning. I greatly feared the presence of these godly people. I prayed and deeply desired. And if ever I got
salvation, I wanted the kind they had.

"One morning during the revival, I went to prayer
meeting with the excuse of going on to the store three
miles away with one of the girls. I had been praying
secretly up in the woods under a tree for God to save
me. How I longed for the burden of sin to be lifted
from my poor lost soul. After the prayer meeting
began, one of the missionaries, who is a Kentucky
girl now laboring for souls in Africa, began to pray.
She started praying definitely for me. Deep conviction struck my soul. The place was awful because of
the presence of God. I was sitting in a chair, but my
knees soon struck the floor and I began pleading
God's mercy. I knew as never before I was lost. I
cried aloud, 'Lord have mercy on me.' My grammar-
school teacher had had us memorize some Scripture.
Among the verses I learned, was 'That if thou shalt
confess with thy mouth the Lord Jesus, and shalt

believe in thine heart that God hath raised him from the dead, thou shalt be saved.' Rom. 10: 9. I prayed and told God just what that verse meant to me and pleaded His mercy. I remember feeling that by God's help I was going with Him and do His will. I didn't care what folks said. Well, I did not get saved that day. I had never seen anyone pray through to salvation, but I knew God had it for me.

"The next day I did not get back to prayer meeting. It was a dry summer, and I took the family washing with the old black iron kettle down to the creek to wash. I would wash awhile and pray awhile. They told me I could get saved right at home if I'd keep on seeking. Next morning I went back to prayer meeting to seek God. I began praying and by the help of the Lord and His faithful workers who instructed me, I found God. They said I could know I was saved. There was not a shadow of a doubt in my mind but that He had saved me. His peace flooded my soul. I stood amazed in wonder as He blessed my heart. Everything was so different. My father and I took the old cross-cut saw over and sawed blocks for the seats.

"Only eternity will tell the results of this one summer of preaching God's Word. I trust I shall be able to tell Jesus just how much I appreciate His love for me and thank Him for bringing salvation to our community. I'm so glad He didn't pass me by. I mean by His grace to do all I can to obey and serve Him.

'But drops of grief can ne'er repay
The debt of love I owe;
Here Lord I give myself away,—
'Tis all that I can do.'

"It was only a short time until the Lord began to impress it deeply on my heart and mind that I ought to preach. At times, I was very happy and blessed about it; at other times, the thoughts of being a woman preacher were anything but pleasant. I knew how prejudiced some of the mountain people were against women preachers. Since that time, I have learned that the first message of the resurrection of Jesus was delivered by a woman, and about many other places in God's Word, where He sets His approval upon the ministry of His hand-maidens.

"I started praying to the Lord to make a way for me to go to school at Mt. Carmel. The missionaries also prayed. My parents were opposed to my going, but I knew God was able to see me through. When the workers went in for camp meeting, I sent my belongings. Then I followed in about two weeks with my suitcase. God was leading. 'The steps of a good man are ordered by the Lord and he delighteth in His way.' Psalm 37:23. Different ones said, 'if you go to Mt. Carmel they will make a preacher out of you.' Little did they know God had already spoken, and was leading me to that end.

"I had been at Mt. Carmel only a few days when I saw my need of being sanctified. I knew very little about the doctrine. But I saw others with the blessing, and I started seeking with a hungry heart. I wanted all God had for me. 'If any man will do His will, he shall know of the doctrine.' John 7:17. I went to the altar and sought, but I did not get the victory. I did all I knew to do but one thing. I was not willing to preach. For a week I reasoned about the matter. Then I told God I would preach, and as I said the last 'yes' the blessing fell. I knew the Holy Ghost had come to abide and all carnality was gone. The Lord did for me far more in that hour than I realized at the time. I was new in the way and knew little of the doctrine. It is so good to know that God can save, sanctify, and establish us in grace.

"How I praise God for a place to prepare for His call and will for my life. I did not have any money. I would go to school at Mt. Carmel during the school year and work there the following summer. The promise the Lord gave me was, 'If ye abide in me, and my words abide in you, ye shall ask what ye will, and it shall be done unto you.' John 15:7. I know if I keep my part of the contract God will keep His.

"I was graduated from Mt. Carmel High School and three years ago I finished my work at the Kentucky Mountain Bible Institute. It has not always been easy. Sometimes I did not have a postage stamp to write home, but God kept me happy and blessed in my soul. 'No good thing will He withhold from them that walk uprightly.' Psalm 84:11. Being the ninth child of a family of ten, I do not mind living the life of a missionary. If I had not minded God I might

not have had as much as I have now, not counting
the joys and blessing of salvation that far surpass
anything temporal. I enjoy my work very much and
would not exchange places with anyone.

"These three years in the pastorate, seeing God
answer prayer and helping people find God, have
been the joy and delight of my soul. I can say with
the song writer, 'Lead on, O King eternal.' 'As for
God, His way is perfect.' I expect to be here laboring
for souls until Jesus comes or He calls me home."

"In the fall of 1936, the Lord opening the way, I
entered the Kentucky Mountain Bible Institute. Jesus saved me in the old-fashioned way after the conditions of repentace, restitution, and faith had been
duly met. It was not difficult to believe unto salvation, when from a penitent heart I truly confessed
my sins. Peace like a river flooded my soul, bringing
a settled consciousness that I was a new creature in
Christ Jesus.

"A few days later, having already seen my need
of a clean heart, in answer to desperate, humble
praying God enabled me to die to the old self-life and
to give my life completely to Him. At that moment
the Holy Ghost suddenly came to His temple, puri-
fying my heart as He said He would in Malachi 3: 1-4.
I truly praise God for His sanctifying power in my
heart and life. It is the enduement with power that
Jesus promised to all who would tarry in prayer for
it; power to live above sin, power to preach His Word,
power to intercede for souls, power to pray for our

material needs. Praise God for His unspeakable gift!

"During my first year in Bible School, as a student pastor, the Lord began talking to me concerning the need of more laborers in this field of service. As soon as His will was known, I said a heart-felt 'Amen' which has brought a lasting peace and a rest of faith.

" 'The Lord, He is God.' His hand is seen to be guiding in the most minute details of His universe. Doesn't He notice the sparrows and through His laws of nature see that they are properly mated? Then He adds, ye are of more value than many sparrows.' Matt. 10: 31. Thus it was in my case. God directed me to a proper mate; one consecrated to Him and to His work through sanctification of the Spirit. She received her training at Mt. Carmel High School and at the Kentucky Mountain Bible Institute.

"During her Senior year at Mt. Carmel, God had sealed to her heart a call into this part of His great vineyard. After her graduation from Bible School we were married. The Lord has now blessed our home with three little boys to raise to His glory. God's benediction is resting upon our home life. He has so many times vindicated that promise, 'Seek ye first the kingdom of God, and His righteousness; and all these things shall be added unto you.' Matt. 6: 33.

"The presence of God in our hearts, and in our home, enables us to believe Him for His presence in our ministry. This is our supreme joy. He has entrusted us with the shepherding of two communities. Among the victories He has given, let us tell of a dear old lady, who as a young girl had given her heart to

Jesus. Her Christian life, she told us, was one of ups and downs. She was so often conscious of inward uprisings that now and then found expression, causing grief to God and grief to her own soul. She would pray over these things until peace would return. In one of our pastoral visits we found her, an invalid, and from all appearance, not able to live much longer. The visit consisted of a song, a season of prayer, and reading a passage of Scripture dealing with heart purity which we felt impressed to read.

"The next day this dear lady sent for us. She desired to hear more about the experience of sanctification. Several of her friends had been called in for a little service which the Lord deigned to bless. During one of our frequent visits to her bedside the Lord graciously met her need in sanctifying her wholly. She is today a happy victorious soul; a blessing to all who visit her; the Lord having added a few more days to her life on earth. In the midst of much persecution she gives this testimony: 'I used to get angry when things did not go my way; and I would have to pray to the Lord to forgive me. Now I feel such a peace; it is so different. I can pray for them that despitefully use me. I am so glad the Lord sent you folk this way to tell me so plainly about this sanctification.' "

"I am so thankful that during my high school days the Lord kept me out of many things that would have ruined my life. It was back there too, that He first let me know that I was to spend my life in His service. I never heard a missionary speak but what my heart was stirred and I wanted to be one.

"The Lord was good to me and let me go to Asbury College, after which I taught school. Two years of public school teaching were enough for me. My heart was hungry for spiritual things and for work which would count spiritually. It was then that I spent part of a summer in the Kentucky hills in the work which Miss McConnell was establishing there. I felt strongly the urge to stay that fall to teach in the Mt. Carmel High School, but since I was still not established in my own personal experience, I was persuaded by circumstances to return to my home.

"Never shall I forget the night when the realization swept over me that I had been taking my own way instead of God's and that was the reason I was so unhappy and dissatisfied. I recall how I admitted it all to Him and told Him that from then on I would mind Him whatever the cost. O, the wonderful relief that came to my soul as I found Him that night so present and ready to forgive me and take me back. Truly, the joy of the Lord became my strength and He enabled me to live for Him in the very community where I had failed Him. It wasn't long until I felt my need to be sanctified, but immediately the enemy brought up everything he could to discourage me, so that I had a long, hard struggle.

"Meanwhile, I felt I must get out to work in order to help my people financially. I got a job in an office, but the longer I stayed the more I wondered why I was there. It was not the work my heart wanted. Finally I quit, and went home. Then I felt badly because I was doing nothing. It was then, that the Lord reminded me of the Kentucky hills! Would I go and trust Him to take care of the things at home? What a struggle ensued! I saw that if I dared fail again I was through. Thank God, He enabled me to say the final 'yes.' What a gracious peace settled down in my soul the night before I left home! I had anticipated feeling so badly about leaving, but He gave me such blessed assurance that I could never doubt I was in the center of His will. That was nearly nine years ago, and I have been happy and satisfied all this time. He has supplied all my needs in every way, besides taking such good care of all the needs at home. Best of all He gave me new light to walk in that enabled me to get things out of my way that had hindered my experience through the years, so that now I know He has saved and sanctified me.

"One day while others were testifying of their calls to Spanish America, the Lord graciously let me see that it was in the hills he wanted me for the rest of my life. By His grace I mean to stay where He wants me and live for Him. I rejoice much in His wonderful salvation that cleanses through and through."

———————

"My first acquaintance with the Kentucky Mountain Holiness Association was made at Romeo, Michigan, camp meeting. I had sought the Lord during the camp of 1938; and a good man there suggested that I should go to the Kentucky Mountain Bible Institute to prepare for the work of the Lord.

"Near the close of my first year as a student of K. M. B. I., I felt led to inquire of the Lord as to His field of service for me. On May 1, 1941, during my devotional hour, I asked the Lord to bless His call to my heart. Almost immediately, the Spirit whispered, 'The mountains shall be thine.' I was concerned that I should not make a mistake, and so I prayed. I said, 'Lord, if this is truly Thy calling, give me a promise.' Again the Spirit said, 'My God shall supply all your need according to His riches in glory by Christ Jesus.' Phil. 4: 19.

"During these past five years, God has graciously fulfilled that promise. The mountains have truly been mine. Away from them, is to be away from home. We have seen the 'iron chariots' of sin destroyed and the Canaanites driven out. It has been a blessing and a means of grace to pray, and then watch God supply every need. The Lord has given us a great field in which to work. The task of soul-winning is great. We are very thankful that our God is able. And I am personally thankful for His saving grace and sanctifying power, and for a definite call into His work."

"With five years of school ahead of me after having been out for ten years; with only three and a half dollars in money; with a timid, backward disposition; and with the dread of leaving my home and loved ones facing me, could I trust God, and go out on His promises? A part of one of my life verses answered the question; 'Fear not, Daniel, for from the

first day that thou didst set thine heart to understand, and to chasten thyself before thy God, thy
words were heard, and I am come for thy words.'

"A desire to work for the Lord and to win souls
for Him became my supreme concern, just as soon
as the Lord saved me from my sins. The urge grew
on me, as the Lord through His wonderful providences led me into the experience of entire sanctification. Scripturally speaking, I was now ready to
work for the Lord. 'And behold, I send the promise
of my Father upon you: but tarry ye . . . until ye be
endued with power from on high.' Luke 24:49. I
had tarried until the Holy Spirit had come and
cleansed my soul, burning out the fleshly mind that
was enmity against God.

"Through the help of the consecrated pastors of
our church, of praying friends there, and of a faithful Missionary Prayer Band group, the Lord worked
and brought an answer to my unspoken prayer; unspoken because I never expected that I would be
granted the glorious privilege of laboring for God in
some special calling. About a year and a half later,
I first heard of this Home Mission field, but of course,
I hardly trusted myself to think of ever even seeing
it, and I surely never prayed that way. The next
time I heard about the work I didn't pass it out of
my thinking so well. Other young people in the
meeting had prospects of getting to go sometime perhaps. They had money, talents, education, and what
I thought it takes to be successful.

" 'O the depth of the riches both of the wisdom and

knowledge of God! how unsearchable are His judgments, and His ways past finding out!' Rom. 11: 33. During the next summer, Miss McConnell held a tent meeting in my home town. During that meeting, through many leadings and providences, God let me know that He wanted me to come. Money, clothing, and encouragement from the Christian people came and in August I put my trunk on the train for the hill country. I was led out as truly as Abraham was led and I knew little more than he did, but I had God's promise, Phil. 1: 6, 'Being confident of this very thing that He which hath begun a good work in you will perform it even until the day of Jesus Christ.'

"The experiences the Lord has brought me through during these nearly twelve years are slowly, but surely getting strength into my soul. It would take a medium-sized book to enumerate even the most outstanding ones. Through days of study, sickness, danger, and sore trials of the soul, as well as times of experiencing 'third heaven' joy, God has kept me. He has seen me through my training in high school and Bible School here and given me the privilege of having a part in almost every phase of the work. God has taken care of my loved ones better than I could ever have hoped to do. What I have learned of God's care in the past causes me to raise my Ebenezer and say, 'Hitherto and Henceforth.' His will is my supreme delight. Is anything too hard for the Lord?"

"One day I read in the Pentecostal Herald an arti-

cle telling about the work of the Kentucky Mountain
Holiness Association. It was all new to me. I felt
that there was a place where people truly knew God
and loved holiness. I longed to be there that I might
learn how to enter the sanctified life and walk
therein. For that reason, I wrote and offered my
services as a teacher in the mission school. After a
few weeks I was accepted. During those weeks I was
much in prayer. One day God met the need of my
heart, and I knew that the precious Holy Ghost had
come and that carnality was cleansed away. I did
not realize that I had a call. I only knew that there
was a pull in my heart to come to the Kentucky
mountains that I might learn more of the things of
God. That was in September, 1936.

"During the three years that followed, there was
a continued restful feeling in my heart and a growing
conviction that God had truly called me there. But
it was on July 9, 1939, that He spoke definitely to my
heart. As I stood by my sister's grave, stunned and
heartbroken by her death in the flash flood, He spoke.
So gently and tenderly He assured me that my precious young sister and I were both in the center of
His will, and that there was where He wanted me to
remain. As I settled it in my heart that I would stay
and continue to answer my call, a deep sweet peace
slipped in underneath the sorrow and I deeply felt
the precious truth that, 'The eternal God is thy refuge and underneath are the everlasting arms.' Deut.
33: 27. My call is precious to my heart and this un-
dergirding of the strength of God is more than suffi-

cient for every need as I humbly do His will from day to day."

"After finishing Bible School, we knew that God had chosen us to be 'stewards of the mysteries of God'; and we also knew that the next step was to come to Asbury College, in Kentucky. Dear friends and others could not understand why we should go from Oregon clear across the country to attend college. Nor could we understand; but we knew God had spoken. We knew also, that to go to any other place, when he had so definitely directed us to come to Asbury, would mean getting ourselves out of the Divine will. In the face of almost impossible circumstances (only money enough to get to Wilmore, Kentucky, with $30 left over; tuition was $60 per quarter at Asbury), we left Oregon and enrolled in Asbury College. The first year was a hard struggle; but we know we were in God's perfect will. He fully supplied our needs through work, kind friends, and through several generous gifts from my own precious father and mother. The Lord had led us to Asbury, in order to lead us to the Kentucky Mountain Holiness Association. Here we met Karl and Bessie Paulo and others from the Mountains; and we found ourselves much in their company and fellowship.

"We were privileged to visit the Kentucky Mountain Bible Institute and Mount Carmel twice while attending Asbury College. How we loved this wonderful work—so warm was the spirit, so powerful the praying, and so holy the lives! We felt we would like to be students again, in the Bible Institute.

"We were seeking the Spirit's guidance as to what we should do when we finished college (December, 1939). The Lord knows so well how to arrange things. Mrs. Swauger and others were visiting Asbury, and she casually said to me, 'Miss McConnell wants you to come up to teach in our Bible School this year.' Those words fell like a cannon ball into my soul, which sent me on a run across the campus, and on two blocks to our apartment, there to hide in the farthest closet corner. I felt my soul would burst with the feeling of unworthiness and inadequacy. To me, it would have been a great privilege to go as a student; but as a teacher—. Perhaps Mrs. Swauger had us confused with someone else, I thought. The more we prayed about the matter, the more blest we were, and the more sure that God was indeed leading us to the mountains.

"How we have delighted in the work and in the precious fellowship of God's sanctified people here. We found it a great blessing to work under Miss McConnell's splendid, sane, spiritual leadership. The Lord blessed and melted our hearts in private devotions, in classes, and in all the work of the Bible Institute; and we found a great love for the students and people in this section springing up within our hearts.

"Then God called us to the Kentucky Mountains for life! Truly, He 'writes His laws in the hearts and minds of His people.' God was calling us to do just exactly what we ourselves would have chosen to do, had the choice been left to us! We will never have words adequate enough to express the joy and blessing and soul-rest that flooded our hearts when the Lord revealed His precious will! How unworthy we felt—and were—for such a ministry; but He encouraged us with the promises from Isaiah 41, 'Fear not, thou worm (and we did feel like we were worms compared with the tremendous responsibility), . . . thou shalt thresh the mountains.' And again with another Scripture: 'Thou shalt yet plant vines upon the mountains.' Thus from day to day, through the Word and the gracious indwelling of the Holy Ghost, we have been sustained, our hearts have kept blest, and God has supplied all our needs. We love God's call, and we praise the Lord many, many times for giving us the privilege of laboring in a truly holiness work with those, who above all else, want to please Jesus in their own lives, and to present others perfect before Him.

"A few times we have been asked to preach in large city churches. We appreciated the opportunity to minister there, but none of those services ever meant as much to us as the times of blessing and victory we have seen in the churches of our Association or in some of the schoolhouses of the Kentucky hills.

"Last summer we held a revival in one of our newer stations in Perry County. One of the best women of the community said ahead of time it wasn't any use to try, for we could never have a revival there. Then God began to answer prayer. How He came upon us as we prayed in the homes and gathered together for the services each night! Before many days this woman testified, 'I never knew that God could work like this!' Although we ourselves have heard of God's power for many years, yet with that woman we would say that before coming into this holiness work in the Kentucky hills we never knew that God could work like this. Now we have seen it with our eyes. And now we thank the Lord for giving us a part in this mighty ministry."

Eternity alone will reveal what my faithful and Spirit-filled co-laborers have accomplished for God and holiness in Eastern Kentucky. I Cor. 3: 9, "For we are laborers together with God." They carry on so nobly year after year, trusting God for all things. Truly God has raised up here or sent into this Home Mission Field, a strong and efficient group of holy men and women who possess great qualities of leadership. I often say that I am the least among them. They carry on and I just follow along after them. My heart-felt appreciation for each one cannot be expressed in words. The work will never cease to accomplish its God-appointed task with this God-called and Holy Ghost-filled corps of laborers. Acts 13: 2, "As they ministered to the Lord, and fasted, the Holy Ghost said, Separate me Barnabas and Saul for the work whereunto I have called them."

Where these workers walk, weep, pray, and minister, the dear people are made to feel their love and to sense God's presence in their midst. Their unselfish, sacrificial lives are winning the precious mountain people to Jesus and thus fulfilling the promise, *"The mountains shall be thine."*

THE END